Getting In Our Own Way:
The Degradation of Student Organizations

By: Johnny Brownlee II

Published by, Johnny Brownlee
Coconut Creek, FL

The stories, scenarios, instances, and people are not representative of any particular people, places, organizations or institutions at any particular time. Some examples given are from confidential sources from around the country at various schools and universities, concerning their school, organization or universities. Some examples are combinations of fact and fiction blended together to create emphasis and protect identities. Resemblance to actual events, people, groups etc. maybe coincidental

Published by: Johnny Brownlee

First Printing: 2013

ISBN-13: 978-0989983006
ISBN-10: 0989983005

Library of Congress Control Number: 2013917343

 Cover Art by: "Artwork courtesy of and copyright Free Range Stock, www.freerangestock.com". Artist name: AirOne

Photography by: Andre Cyrus

Proofreaders: Roxanne De Freitas,
Mikerlande "Mickey" Erilus,
Anioushka Guillame,
Alvin Johnson,
Rachel Mondesir,
Te'Chaunta Richardson,
Rochelle Spencer,
Tharisa Walker

Getting In Our Own Way

Dedication

I dedicate this book to leaders, past present and future.
To those brave enough to speak up for change. This is for
those who refuse to use their age or status as a crutch.
To those that don't know they can fail, and refuse to do so
or accept the status quo. This is for those that are crazy
enough to believe they can change the world and bold
enough to try.

About the Author

Johnny Brownlee is a national speaker and workshop presenter.
He has held numerous leadership positions in various organizations, school and statewide. He is the former two time Director of Florida Atlantic University's former agency, Black Student Union & Multicultural Programming. An organization that at the time was one of the largest and best-funded student organizations in the nation, with 600+ members and six-figure budgets, at a transitioning mostly commuter school, on a campus of between approximately 20 and 25 thousand, with 12-15% black student population.

While in college he helped develop programs and create events, and continually fought for student and multicultural rights, while actively being involved in a number of clubs and organizations. He often speaks on student involvement, community involvement, leadership and civic engagement. He is considered to be extremely proficient in areas concerning student participation, student organization, student interaction and Student Government, along with consulting for students, advisors and administrators.

You can visit and book Johnny at his website
www.onemanmanytalents.com

Find him on Facebook at
www.facebook.com/onemanmanytalents

Getting In Our Own Way

Acknowledgements

I want to first thank God for giving me the courage and strength to write this book and leading me through the process. Thank God also for guiding me through these experiences, seeing the lessons and possibilities, gaining wisdom and insight, and having the mindset to want to help others.
I'd like to thank my family and friends for showing me support and encouraging me to push on when the road got rough, thank you for pushing me, giving advice, continued prayers and being a listening ear. Thank you for your knowledge, wisdom and understanding. Special thanks to mom, grandma & granddad, aunt Freda and aunt Janie, no one supports like y'all. Special Thanks to my big little cousin Amos, without you a lot of behind the scenes things either get delayed or not done at all. We are in this together. Thank You. And my biggest cheerleader, my little sister Qui, thanks to you for your support.

Thanks Mr. Hasani Pettiford, for hammering home the importance of this book being wrote and encouraging me to get started at once.

To my friend and my brother Devin T. Robinson X, thank you for everything we will continue to change the world together.

I want to thank my mentor Mr. Ancel Pratt III, you have played a crucial role in helping me with the book, and had it not been for you, I would have never got involved in student leadership. So thank you.

To Mr. Alex Saint-Louis, thank you for forcing me to be brave as a leader and using me as an instrument of change.

I also have to thank Mr. Benjamin Dixon for your eagerness to help, advice, suggestions, and encouragement.

I want to thank: Roberto Roy, Dayna Smith, Jerson Dulius, Brendy Dorieus, Keisha Carter, Mickerlande "Mickey" Erilus, Deborah Francisque, Kweku Darfoor, Collene O'Reilly, Roxanne De Freitas, Dwayne Hunt, Rachel Mondesir, Diangleo Frazer, Kerri Ann Nesbeth, and all of the other countless student leaders and former student leaders that contributed to this book. There are a number of leaders and advisors, both current and former from schools across the nation, who were unwilling to have their names mentioned, but your stories, suggestions, advice and insight was invaluable and is represented. Thank You

I want to thank all of the clubs and organizations I've been apart of at one point or another. The experiences I gained from being a participant or leader in each, allowed me to be able to speak and teach today, the experiences are invaluable and the relationships I've been able to build through them unbreakable. I want to thank Florida Atlantic University Black Student Union, formerly Black Student Union & Multicultural Programing, Konbit Kreyol, Caribbean Student Association, Association of Latin American Students, NAACP, Program Board, Home Coming Committee, SPICE, Konbit Kreyol Alumni Association, National Society of Black Engineers, and every other organization that I've worked with, joined, or supported.

I've served on a number of executive boards, every single person I've served with I've learned something from. I must send a special thank you to each and every member of the e-boards that I was privileged to lead. I acknowledge that I'm by no means perfect, and that I was sometimes hard to work with, but I hope that it was all worth it. I hope you understood the passion I had for changing things, being professional, and the bigger picture of our organizations. We're a family for life. We'll be forever connected in history together. We accomplished so much together, if only we knew then what we know now, we would've accomplished so much more. If we had this book we'd have ran the world. To the general members we lead, thank you for your passion, hard work, and belief that we could change things and set a new standard. We did! I dedicate this book to that era of leaders and workers at a small developing school most had never heard of, with a group of student that wanted to change their school, communities and the world. We had so much discipline and were so cutting edge and a number of us saw the bigger picture, stepped forward to do so and continue to make changes in the world in various sectors. To the various other similar groups and clubs we interacted with during that era, at numerous conferences, this is for you also. You helped show us what else was possible besides having a large budget.

My advisors during my student involvement: Mr. Chambers, Mr. Marc Davis, Mrs. Raquel Grant, Mrs. Byrd, Mrs. Lisa Bardill, Mrs. Rivka Felsher, Ms. Gayle Evans, Mrs. Cathy Webb and Dr. Abass, thank each of you for everything.

Last but not least, you the reader, and supporter. Thank you for demanding this book, supporting this book, and thank you to each and every conference and school that has contacted me and allowed me to speak, teach and consult with you. I truly appreciate you taking the

initiative to want to improve your organizations,
I pray you realize you can change more than just your
organization and your school campus.

Anyone I forgot to name, blame my head not my heart, I
thank each and every one of you, one by one, name after
name, group after group.

Getting In Our Own Way

Table of Contents

Getting In Our Own Way

Introduction

All around the country, many of our student organizations are suffering from a lack of funds, participation, care, and involvement. There seems to be a civil war between old school and new school members, and because of this, our organizations are resorting to harmful and drastic measures that go against the purpose and principles on which the organizations were founded. Student organizations have definitely lost something that earlier generations possessed.

Organizations no longer have the activism and sacrifice of groups from the 60's and 70's, drive of the 80's organizations, the urgency of the 90's or money and participation of organizations from the early 2000's. In the early 2000's, there was an explosion in participation & activism, with many groups experiencing record numbers of participants and receiving record funding. Then the recession came, institutions made budget cuts, the money went, but so did the participation. What happened? We seek to see if it is a generational apathy problem, a leadership problem or are other factors the problem.

This book is written based on a lot of pain, aggravation, struggles and misunderstandings. These are lessons learned from experiences as a student leader and examples shared with me at various colleges and conferences as a speaker and workshop presenter.

A spectrum of student organizations are represented in the chapters to come; various sizes, types, budget levels, make ups, experience levels, at public and private institutions.

While there are a number of other problems not covered by this book, and the problems at each school are unique in severity, these are the most encountered and comprehensive issues student organizations often meet. These are lessons learned by various organizations by trial and error, from success and tragic failure. From continued improvement to a gradual decline, organizations known in national circles, to underdog organizations that continue to thrive against all odds. From groups held in high esteem, to sharp falls from grace, and organizations that are less than 5 years old, to organizations possibly older than you.

If your organization is blessed enough to have none of these issues, or to have never dealt with these issues, take this as a cautionary tale and opportunity to plan ahead if they ever become an issue.
If your organization is/was dealing with any of the issues outlined in this book. I pray you will find the answers and strength needed to get your organization on track.
We seek to figure out what factors are currently costing us members, stability, funding, involvement and respect of our former members, founders, elders and in some cases our institutions. Especially, since many universities don't archive, catalog or keep records on student clubs and organizations. We aim to find out is it a generational problem, educational, or do we take the power, prestige, and responsibility of student organizations and student involvement for granted.

The Knowledge Problem........ What Kind of Organization are We?

In most student organizations, the first acknowledgment of their being an issue in the organization usually happens when older members and younger members begin having a civil war of sorts, over the current direction of the organization and/or the type of events that they normally throw.

Usually, the older generation wants to keep things traditional and conservative and do things the way they've always been done in the organization. The younger members are usually hungry for change, they want to modernize, change the focus and update the way things are done. The younger generation usually think's they can do things better and are interested in finding a way to have more fun and not make things as serious, ritualistic or formal.

The older generation and the younger generation usually embody two different and conflicting philosophies on what is considered fun and appropriate for the organization. Any organization that wants to stay relevant has to update, and change with the times, but they don't have to change completely and to the detriment of their organization. They have to stay true to what they are and what their true purpose is.

Often time's younger members see the fun the older generations had and misinterpret it.

3

They see when the executive board lets their hair down and relaxes a little bit. However, they don't see or understand the work that went into being able to have that fun. A lot of younger members don't understand that you work hard and play hard, but that it's not all fun all the time, neither is it all fun most of the time for an executive board. The fun that executive board members often have together is about more than just the bonds of friendship they build, it's enjoying the moment that had to be fought for, for as long as it last, because they will need to fight again later for another moment for the club to enjoy later.

Many student leaders today, often seek popularity and numbers rather than substance, and it's a nationwide issue. They want numbers and popularity yet they receive neither, nor substance, nor are they taken seriously. It's amazing at what's considered being a successful organization these days because it so hard to get people to care or be involved.

When trying to decide whether to go the old way or the new way for events, the answer can usually be found in the middle by posing this simple question and answering it honestly, **what kind of Organization are we**?

In The Knowledge Problem, people within our organizations often don't know the basic information an alleged member should be familiar with, in order to say they are apart of a group. Let's call them interview questions; because they are the first things someone that is not familiar with the organization would ask and expect you to be able to tell them so that they can get a better understanding of what this organization is about. If the student newspaper or local radio wanted to do a story on your group, these are things they would ask first. Simple, surface knowledge questions. Yet all too often members of our organizations can't answer surface questions, neither in-depth questions about the organizations we so claim to love and be a part of. We have failed to realize that love is an action verb, and in order to express it and show it, we have to do things for our organization and know things about it.

We can usually determine and settle what kind of events and initiatives we should be taking on, just by answering that one question. **What kind of Organization are we?** Is this a social organization? Is it a political organization? Is this a religious organization, an advocacy organization? Is it a cultural organization or a historical organization, but what kind is it? There is a possibility it's a hybrid group. Is this a social-political organization or religious-political? Cultural-historical? Possibly we have a few events or should plan some events that are purely about entertainment and fun. We don't need to be militant, educational or drab at all times. But at our core, **What Kind of Organization are we?**

After that, what are our founding principles? What are we based on, what are our guidelines? Is this organization based on religious values, ancient principles, Kwanzaa Principles, principles of liberty? What are the qualities that describe the people in this organization and what they are about? Is it love, peace, and humanitarian aid, or scholarship, unity and justice?

What is this organization's Motto? What's the mission statement? What's the vision statement? What's the organization's purpose? Who do you serve? Who do our events cater to? What's your demographic?

What are the specified duties of the executive board members? What are the duties and rights of the general members? What is the process and conditions under which the general members can impeach a member of the executive board?

Anybody at random in your organization should be able to answer any of these types of questions, and not just the executive board and advisor. Anybody with a t-shirt, any member sitting in your meeting, or claiming to be a part of the organization should be cognizant of those very basic things.

Too many people in our organizations today can't answer those types of questions. Honestly, a lot of advisors and executive board members can't even answer those questions. The reason why, because most people serving on executive boards, many advisors and a large majority of members have never read their organization's constitution. The answer to all of those questions should be contained in the constitution. Most conflicts can be solved by just being well versed on what the constitution contains and says about the issue. Depending on the age of the organization the constitution will not answer every question or solve every dispute, but it lends us perspective and gives us a starting point of how to address the issue. The constitution puts us in a frame of mind of how to think about addressing the organizations issues, because it's not only what's stated in the constitution, but also what's not stated, and what's implied that matters.

How can you carry on the great tradition and legacy that the founders left for you without even knowing what they intended for the organization? Event and directional issues, in addition to people just taking it upon themselves to change things they don't like, understand or find limiting, can often be prevented by everyone understanding what the intent of this organization is. Another condition within The Knowledge Problem is that often time's people within student organizations do not acknowledge the founders. They don't know anything about the founders of the organization. Who's vision made this even possible for you to have this outlet, brotherhood, or family atmosphere? Who were they? What's their history? What were their associations? What were their personal beliefs?

Those types of questions tell us why we should honor them, but they also answer deeper questions about ourselves, and why we wish to join this type of association. Why we wish to be a part of a group is something many of us are never forced to contemplate. We're rarely asked to think about it that deeply or to be that honest. What are our true intentions? Is it for resume purposes, because we're bored and it's just something to do? Is it because everybody else was doing it, or do we truly believe in the purpose of the organization and want to be associated with men and women that think like the founders? With the exception of fraternal organizations, most student organizations (student governments included) don't know, and are never required to know anything about their founders and show them little if any reverence. Most organizations don't even celebrate their founders' day, but in order to do that, you'd have to know when it is. And a lack of reverence for the founders makes it easy for people who don't know about the organization to suggest radical and outlandish changes and feel comfortable and justified in doing so.

Finally, possibly the biggest issue in the Knowledge Problem is that many of the leaders in student organizations currently possess little or no training. There are too many people in leadership positions doing jobs and holding responsibilities for which they do not have qualifications, training, or knowledge of how to execute the requirements of said position. The reason for this lack of knowledge is because way too often, the outgoing leadership or outgoing executive board, or committee heads, do not train members in the ways and duties of

the organization before they become leaders.
And once elections happen, often times the exiting leaders
do not take time to train the next set of leaders to assure
they acquire basic knowledge and tricks of the trade
about how to run the organization. There is far too often
not enough of an exchange of information between the
outgoing administration and incoming one.

At all levels of business, government etc., there are
requirements for holding certain positions, you start one
place and work your way up through the system.
However, in our student organizations, this appears to be
a foreign concept, a person can go from doing nothing to
being president. And once that person wins presidency
there will be no debriefing between the outgoing and
incoming officer. Many new officers get elected and they
wish to start implementing their vision, their goals for the
year.

However, the first thing a new officer should do and needs
to do is assure that there is no unfinished business from
the previous administration or anything that may
interfere with new administration's plans. Did the
outgoing executive board make any deals that the
incoming board will be held to? Did they leave the
organization with a budget surplus and maybe you can
do a few extra things? Or worse, did they leave a deficit
that the new administration will have to take care of, and
then reevaluate the remaining budget? Did the outgoing
executive board leave the organization with a good name
or bad name business wise? Is the new executive board
going to have to mend some broken relationships or prove
that things will be different this year? Basically, what is
the state of the organization? A full Strength, Weakness,
Opportunity, and Threats (S.W.O.T.) analysis needs to be
shared because there are things the president is
conscious of about the organization and operation that no
one else knows. And the same for every other position,

there are things the secretary knows, no one else knows, there are things the CFO/treasurer knows that no one else knows and the incoming person needs to be savvy to those things, to make the transition as smooth and as consistent as possible. If the last executive board did a good job, you want to be able to pick up where they left off, and elevate rather than write an entirely new chapter. You want to learn from their mistakes so you don't have to learn them and make them. If the last executive board was bad, you want to know what they did, why it didn't work, and now you can devise a strategy for how you can approach situations differently. Experience may be the best teacher, but something's you should not want to have to experience. Anyone can learn from their mistakes, but wise people learn from other people's mistakes also.

One of your first priorities as a new executive board is to make this year better than last, especially in a year that was a setback. You want to have continued progress. Take the knowledge and set goals for the upcoming year that are:

Specific (Who? What? When?)
Measurable (How will I know when it's accomplished, or progress is being made?)
Attainable (Do you have the means to complete the Goal?)
Realistic (Will this stretch you? Do you believe you can do it?)
Timely (Is there a deadline?)

Knowledge is power, but applied knowledge is exponentially more powerful.

Getting In Our Own Way

The Historical Problem

The reason a lot of student organizations are in transition or experience changes into something they were never intended to be is because the people in the organizations possess no knowledge of, sense of, or respect for the organization's history. And in too many cases, people don't care to learn the history. Very few members actively seek out their history.

Besides not knowing founders, many current students are unfamiliar with anyone who predates their time in the club. There are student organizations across the country that are decades old, yet the current membership cannot name any former members in the organization who predates the four to five years that they were active in the organization. That is almost spitting on legacies. That's taking for granted the literal blood, sweat, tears and sacrifices the people before you dealt with in order for your organization to even exist. All of the struggles, all of the battles are just forgotten, never acknowledged and in too many cases never even known about.

In addition to the events or issues, what about the people? Who was a part of this organization and how did they contribute? Who were the other pioneers? The most important people to ever be a part of your organization are often times not the founders, but the people that supported the founding vision, carried it forward or

11

enhanced it. Their legacy deserves respect, admiration and to be remembered also.

But it's not just admiration; there are great lessons to be learned by knowing who was in your organization. Who fought for this organization? Who came up with these events and initiatives that we still participate in? Who was the best leader? What made them the best? Who was worst and Why? The worst leader may not have been terrible or ill equipped; they may have been great for their time and far better than anyone currently. They may be the worst in comparison to all of the other excellent men and women that were apart of your organization. You may have a situation where if John Doe is your worst president ever, then everyone else has to be great even to be considered a bad president. What if you inherit a legacy of all excellent, transcendent, progressive presidents? Wouldn't you want to be aware of that? Who are these people that made it possible for you and I to be a part of something like this, at this institution, in this day and time? There are two types of leaders, anointed leaders and appointed leaders, and strong organizations recognize and appreciate the value of both. Appointed leaders are selected or elected, anointed leaders do not require a title, in order to lead, hold influence and sometimes be the glue of an organization.

Even the things that may be trivial tell a story about how your organization has evolved. Who is the youngest, oldest, first female, or first minority to hold certain positions? If it's a culture specific club, has any one not of that culture held office or joined the club? What struggles, conflicts, and experiences have we had to overcome, whether they be within ourselves, with the administration, or with other clubs/organizations? These types of things tell us a story of how our organization has transformed over the years.

We may not have always been as progressive and open minded as we are now, and knowing these things help us understand where we've come from, where we may want to return to or ensure that we never return to those days or behaviors. Knowing these things can point out trends, that maybe we need to work on before the trend becomes a problem. We could be making history (positive or negative), and not realize it. The group could be repeating history; we could be going through something that could've been avoided. We could be replicating or surpassing the greatest moments our club has known. Our history is a measuring stick; it lets us know how special we are, or how much harder we need to work.

As well as people and events, the modern student participant in today's student organizations know next to nothing of their organization's traditions. Every organization has traditions; traditions are what make organizations an institution. No matter how small or seemingly insignificant, everything we do has a meaning and/or reason. Trust and believe there is a specific reason why we follow this ritual at the beginning of every event. We may have meetings every other week, always at a specific time, always in a specific room or building for a reason. What is it? The official colors of the organization are as follows because... What do these symbols on our logo mean? Does their placement symbolize specific meaning or value specific to this organization? Why do we do this event, every year, at this particular time of year? Is there a specific reason we don't hold this event ever year and instead do it every third year? How did this become one of our traditions?

Traditions are always deeper than, "I'm not sure, that's the way we've always done it." Well, Why? What if we didn't always do it that way? What if we had a different way of doing things before this one, what sparked that change and who instituted that change? How do these traditions define us? Traditions are important because they are what make the organizations and the experiences had in them unique.

The Historian

Do you know what the most important and most undervalued position on any executive board is? The Historian, almost hands down because they archive information. A lot of people will disagree with that assessment because in most organizations the historian is a fairly easy position, and many organizations have never had a dynamic historian. In many organizations, the historian is allowed to possess little, if any history about the organization, and do an incomplete job the entire year. The weakest link on many executive boards, the person that just wants to hold a leadership role, the person that was placed in a position because it was open, the position nobody was really running for, can often be found in the historian slot. Why? Because in many organizations, we've convinced people that the historian's role is marginal, that the workload is light, and that being the historian is easy. In fact, many organization's expectations of the historian are to show up at events, take a few pictures, and compile them for the slide show presentation at the end of the year banquet, and essentially that's about it, sadly. And how good of a historian they were is based solely on how good the slide show was and how quick were they able to get pictures of events up on the website and social media pages.

The Historian's job is grander than it is used for, it requires so much more work, and has way more responsibility than allowed, perceived or advertised. To even do the historian's job requires a special person. The historian has to be someone that really truly and honestly loves the organization and has a thirst to learn

14

and share everything possible about it. The historian should be one of the foremost experts on your organization. The job of the historian is to know and share in detail; what is, what was, and what should be. And through words, pictures, video, etc. show and answer the questions, who, what where, when, why and how? The historian should be informing us about what's the back-story of the organization, past, and present. Where have we been, and in what direction are we headed? The Historian should also be the archivist; they should be making some sort of history book, yearbook, legacy book, or maybe even a time capsule. What's the pulse of the nation, what's the pulse of the school, what's the pulse of this organization? 1, 5, 10, 20 years down the road someone should be able to pick up your history book and feel as if thcy somewhat understand what was going on and relate. Who were the members, who were the advisors, what were the accomplishments, what were the struggles/ battles? What was the social and political climate?

If you don't think that current events have a profound impact on the membership or types of events that organizations throw, I dare you to pay attention to the type of events that were going on before and after events like Hurricane Katrina, 9/11, the Election of Barack Obama and Occupy Wall Street. I guarantee that student organization events reflect the politics of the time. Years down the line we should be able to look back and compare the past and present, year to year.

   The historian should be a good leader and team player, because to do a thorough job, they definitely need a committee. Your historian should always be working, because your organization's history is a living, breathing thing. The historian should be working from the day they take office to the last day they are in it, possibly slightly before and slightly beyond.

The historian should always be vocal when decisions are made. For example, "Mr. Chairman/ Madam Chairwoman the reason why we do that event annually is to honor the memory of three members of this organization who all passed in that year, I think it would be prudent that we keep that event, we've been doing it for the past 15 years. It's not about how many people show up, it's about honoring their memories." Or another possible example, " Since the inception of this organization, we've never thrown that type of event, because they go against our core principles, I don't think that's a precedent this executive board should set", " The constitution was changed in 2002 on a 4-3 vote, because this very circumstance arose."

A silent historian is one that doesn't know their job, and a vocal historian will make sure your executive board, administration, and organization end up on the right side of history, and that is invaluable. Your historian needs to be strong. Strong enough to stand up and defend the history against anybody, but also strong enough to fairly and accurately report history, whether it be good or bad, whether they agree or disagree. While a part of the executive board, the historian needs to be able to report with impunity, and honest enough to self-report and whistle blow, because history doesn't judge us all delicately.

Historical Role

If you're lucky, in most organizations someone may know or know who they can ask when the organization was founded and a few choice accomplishments, selling points and bragging rights of the organization. But deeply embedded in The Historical Problem is that many people in student organizations today don't know their organization's historical role. Meaning, what honors or awards have been bestowed upon this organization? Most don't know the organization's resume. What have we accomplished and affected at the University, in the local area or possibly in the nation? Have we been Organization of the Year? Best New Organization? Maybe we've logged the most community service hours in a year before, or been the organization with the highest GPA. Has this organization ever raised the most money for a cause or won a competition? Maybe you've been the largest, or longest surviving since a certain time period. What if your organization was given the key to the city or some other huge honor? Has the organization been recognized by the mayor or other officials? Have you ever won homecoming activities? Many organizations don't know many things that they can hang their hats on and be proud of their organization for. Not knowing these things affects the pride we feel for the organization.

You'd be surprised at what student organizations can accomplish and what advancements they have been directly involved in. Some student organizations have made huge social impacts on campus and abroad. Was your student organization involved in a protest or a rally of some kind? Your student organization could be the reason why color lines were broken at your school, hence the reason why certain classes may be offered, an increased number of faculty, staff, and students of color exist. Your organization could be the reason why diversity is celebrated at your campus. Your organization could be the reason they serve a particular type of food now in the cafeteria or have certain accommodations in the residence halls. Your organization could have participated in something truly historical, a number of movements have been lead and issues fought for and brought to the light by students.

The American Youth Congress who fought against racial discrimination in the 1930's and the Student Nonviolent Coordinating Committee of the 60's played an integral part of the Civil Rights Movement. They participated in the Freedom Rides, Freedom Summer, and in protesting the Vietnam War. For better or worse, the Student Nonviolent Coordinating Committee, American Youth Congress, Black Panther Party, National Student Association, Student for a Democratic Society, and United We Dream were each student organizations, long before they were national organizations or movements.

The Civil Rights Movement, Darfur, protest against various wars, human trafficking, HIV/AIDS to name a few, have all been issues lead or had students at the forefront of them. If your organization participated in a historic protest or a sit-in for civil rights, lobbied or spoke in front of the government about an issue, isn't that something to be proud of and shouldn't it be remembered and cherished forever? The legendary shutting down the administrative buildings, blocking the campus entrance, and the students having a sit-in to protest stories we here about in books and movies; that type of stuff gives you a sense of responsibility, and it gives aspirations. It puts in focus the whole legacy that has been left in place.

The things you go through, the things you change, the people you help, the lives that benefit from your organization's work, that history and legacy needs to be cataloged, remembered and taught.

Getting In Our Own Way

The RESPECT Problem

The most baffling issue for student organizations today is the lack of respect they garner. There exist a lack of respect from our own members. In many cases, the lack of respect introduces itself during hard times for the organization, usually when the organization is going through some sort of rough transition or decline. People have a lack of knowledge and no sense of history because they don't fully respect the organizations they belong to. People attempt to make changes to our organizational structures because they don't fully respect the organization. People attempt to go against our core principals and values when they don't respect our organizations.

Think about it, one would never walk into a military organization, an alumni organization, a fraternal order or any other organization steeped in history and tradition and attempt to start changing the colors, the motto, the events, the rules etc. A change in leadership or influence that takes our history and traditions and disregards them only happens from lack of respect. A leadership group that decides to forgo cultural, service and educational activities so they can focus on more social and fun activities only does so because they feel as if they can get away with it and because they feel as if it's not that serious/important for a general student organization. If that change is made, the people that made it will not be around to help get the organization back on track

It is essential to know what the reputations of our organizations are, and maintain them or fix them; so that we are always seen in the way we wish to portray ourselves. You teach people how to respect your organization based on what you accept and do not accept, and how your members conduct themselves. Respect and reputation go hand in hand, you should always be aware of your organization's reputation amongst members, administrators, and vendors; it makes a world of difference in how they treat you. Your organization's reputation is the sum of your claims minus what people say and think about your organization. *(Your Organizations claim – What others say and think about you = Organization's Reputation)*

The respect has to start in-house, even when it comes to what may seem like little things. We must respect our own authority figures, history and processes of our organizations. The little things are the big things, and we ought to learn to respect the signs, symbols, colors and traditions of our organizations. Consider this, Greeks respect their letters and paraphernalia, soldiers respect their uniform, and police respect their shield; so much to the fact that everyone else respects those things. When we see people in those types of organizations disrespect their organization we as outsiders get disgusted and we believe it reflects negatively on the whole organization. We need to take that into consideration when it comes to general student organizations also. Regardless of whether it's a t-shirt, jacket or dog tag, our members should know to respect our organizations the same way. When you wear your t-shirt you represent the whole organization and so does your conduct. If everyone else is afraid of embarrassing the organizations they belong to, general student organization members should be also.

The disrespect for our organizations usually manifests itself during hard times and periods of decline, because organizations often get desperate for members, new ideas, events, etc. and we allow our standards to relax. We begin to accept and do things in our organization that would have never been permissible or acceptable at any other point in time. When we get desperate, all too often we'll gamble the entire organization's fate and reputation. We become too fixated on the quantity of our members, rather than the quality of our members

One of the clear signs of desperation in an organization is when we start using gimmicks to advertise our club and it's events. I.e. advertising free food and giveaways, things that we hope will drum up extra excitement and interest in our club. We focus on things that will bring extra bodies through the door, rather than appreciate the people that are there and are genuinely interested in the program or organization, the true quality members.

Multiple generations of members have learned to judge the worthiness of an event based on how many or what groups of people are going to be in attendance. Events have become places to be seen, rather than events to support, get educated or just enjoy. 15 people that really want to be at the event and get something out of it, is better than 200 people that showed up because they had nothing better to do. The sad thing is most people talk about being leaders when in actuality they are followers. They are usually worried about who's doing, who did, and who will see them doing and judge them for it. So when we use gimmicks we set ourselves up for disappointment and failure. Going into the event, we're aware that if the gimmick works, the majority of people will only show up for the food/giveaways and as soon as those are given out they will proceed to leave the event, or not show up to another event until those types of things are advertised again. Do you really expect someone to respect or be interested in your organization when we use gimmicks to sell it?

Another issue within The Respect Problem is that members in the organizations often don't recognize their own power. We have these strong words that describe our clubs; union, association, organization, incorporation, sisterhood, brotherhood; yet we treat them as if they are toys. We title our organizations these types of words then have the audacity to not uphold those titles by not being unified, associated with anything of greatness, organized, business-like or family like. What gives us the right?

Many of us only see our student organization as something that's four years of our life and social. We think of our organizations in terms of all fun, not business. Which couldn't be further from the truth, when you are in a leadership position in a student organization, you are essentially running a non-profit organization. We underestimate our experiences. The skills you gain from these opportunities are transferrable, and experiences that can and will serve you forever. Just by being on an executive board or the head of a committee, you learn a number of skills that are applicable to the job world and your resume. Being in the average student organization you gain; management experience, budget experience, negotiation experience, hiring and firing experiences, team building experience, programming and event planning experience, just to name a few.

Here's an example, I was the director of an organization with 600 members. I had an executive board of about 10 and 5 committee heads. I had a paid position and we started with about 20 members. That is management and team building because I had hiring and firing responsibilities, it was my job that if someone was not doing their duties to get rid of them or replace them with someone else. We grew from 20 participants to 600, that requires marketing. Most jobs I'd apply for after graduation, the companies wouldn't even have 600 employees. Regardless of the size of your organization that's management experience. My organization had a six-figure budget for programming, we were responsible for not only writing that budget so it could be approved but also for managing that budget throughout the year. Whenever we wanted to put on a conference, throw an event or book a speaker/performer we had to budget and negotiate the contracts. I was also a brand manager; your organization has a name and reputation. We have a professional reputation amongst booking agencies, vendors and performers. They expect that we will be professional, they will be paid in a timely manner, all parts of our agreement will be honored, and any problems will be handled in a timely manner. If I wrote a letter of recommendation for someone, whether it is for grad school, a job on campus, or for their profession, we have a reputation of producing quality people. We have a 40+ years reputation on campus for being organized, professional and years of rapport with outside vendors, which builds and maintains respect and credibility.

When a company would tell me it's just student government experience or a student organization, I'd take exception with that and explain, that it's more than you're giving us credit for, it's real taxpayer money and real laws and consequences stand behind the allocation and usage of that money. And the same things are true for your organization and experiences also, put your leadership experiences on your resume. People need to respect your organization, what's required to run a student organization and your experiences gained by doing so.

When you join; a Greek letter organization, Student Government Association, Resident Student Association, or if you are governor of your campus, president of the student body, you often learn about all of the celebrities, government officials and titans of industry that were apart of those organizations or held those positions. Yet rarely do we get that same courtesy in general student organizations. Which connects us back to The Historical Problem, because if we don't know who else was in organizations like ours and if we aren't proud enough to tell people, then we won't have Titans of Industry and successful people to talk about of our own, because everybody is not going to pledge, or be a Residence Hall Coordinator, or Student Body President. By us not underestimating and respecting our experience in general student organizations, it makes it so that other organizations and employers have to respect us also, because it's not just fun, it's business. There are successful people affiliated with general organizations also.

However, if our student groups are going to get the respect they deserve from being business like, then we need to treat them as businesses, and it starts with how we choose leaders and representation. In many of our organizations, we don't possess a healthy respect for the election/ appointment process. Most elections in student organizations on any level are little more than a popularity contest. Members often vote for their friends, rather than who is most qualified and willing to do the work. Being one of the leaders of an organization is about getting stuff done, not about popularity. So our friends need to know that whom we vote for is business, never personal.

It's cool to see friends in positions or have one on the board along with you; it can make the experience very fun. But if they didn't care, work, and participate as a general member, then more responsibility is probably not what they need.

Speaking of responsibility let's talk about three words we don't use often enough to show we mean business as leaders; fire, impeach and resign. We talk about being business, but we often times hold on to people or positions out of pride, ego or fear of looking like the bad guy, and end up letting the organization suffer. In business, if a person can't produce or do what's required, they are let go. In jobs that require passion and motivation, if you don't have it, you are let go. It should be the same way in our organizations. In your personal lives, if being in the organization is truly requiring too much of your time and taking away from your studies or other responsibilities, or if you just don't have the time or desire to do an adequate job, resign. Why hold on to a position, if it affects you, or your performance negatively? And as leaders, why hold on to people that affect and reflect the organization negatively?

In addition to business, many people in our student organizations today do not respect the networking possibilities that exist. It does not require hundreds of years in existence, and a national organization to network. Regardless of the size of your organization, you can network within your organizations. You can create brotherhood/ sisterhood, and family bonds also. On day one of joining an organization, I was a part of, we would let it be known that you were joining a family. We will be there for your graduation, we'll be there for your first job, we'll be there for your wedding, and if we outlive you, we'll be the ones to memorialize you. And as time has gone by, I have been a part of each of those scenarios.

Some of my best friends are people I met in a general student organization. Once again, because your student organization deserves to be treated as more than just four years and social, the networking we did, created a family aspect. The networking begins on a college level then you just expand it and grow with it as you grow.

For instance, the members of your organization can study together or help each other out with assignments, to hold each other accountable. Maybe set a goal to be the organization with the highest grade point average on campus. Then set up study groups for people with the same/ similar majors. Maybe they can study for a big standardized test relevant to their major together i.e. LSAT, GRE, MCAT. You can also set up study groups and encourage those that are strong in one area to help those who are weak in other areas. For example, if your club has engineers, accountant, and/or science majors, they can help explain and tutor members that are weak in science and math. Your political science, sociology, English majors can help teach others how to research, write and review papers etc. So we began to build bonds and network right there within our student organization, after all, it is extracurricular activity, correct? And people can network around similar interest if you have some exercise science majors or people that personal train, they can help people that are interested in getting fit, eating healthy and they can work out together. Get people together and start an intramural team for your club. These are extracurricular activities, however, the majority of what you learn in college is learned outside the classroom from the experiences you have and the people you interact with. You learn life skills outside of the classroom. Things like this don't have to stop after you graduate.

One of the saddest parts in The Respect Problem is the lack of respect we hold for the alumni of our organizations. In greek letter organizations, societal organization and other pledge organizations the alumni are praised for being around, but in general student organizations, we shun them. It seems to be a belief that after you graduate, you should go about your business. In other types of organizations you'd never think to curse at alumni and tell them to get a job and family, and tell them what they can and can't do anymore. But I've heard plenty of stories of it happening. People in student organizations today don't want alumni to have an opinion or any say so, and it's the reason a lot of our organizations have little or no direction. No one older is around to pull them back to the center and inform them that this organization is changing for the worst, compared to when they were a member, it's getting a little out of hand in this area. But a lot of people once they graduate have no interest in still being apart or giving back to their organizations. Why?

Why is it not ok for your alumni, to come back and check in on the organization? Why is it not ok for you when you graduate to go back and check in or help out your organization? Why is it not encouraged, it's a part of networking? Why can't you after graduating and getting a job, decide to go back and help your organization? You know what the issues were when you were in school and a part of the organization, so why can't you help? We can easily go back to our organizations and sponsor or contribute to an event because the budgets are low. We can sponsor the t-shirts, sponsor food for an event. You as an alumnus can sponsor a few people to go to a conference. If you want to put conditions on your gift, you'll only sponsor people with a certain GPA or that attended a
certain number of the organization's events.

A number of alumni can get together and start a scholarship for members in the organization. There are a number of things alumni of a student organization can do. If you're aware of opportunities or internships you can help inform or recommend the current members of your organization.

An alumnus could be a mentor and provide valuable advice, on an organizational level, life level, and career level. Why shouldn't we help each other if we are apart of the same organization? If you're an alumnus why can't you return for special events like homecoming, the organization's founders day, anniversaries, or end of the year banquet? Why do we feel as if we shouldn't, it's perfectly acceptable for pledge organizations, why not ours? We hear of people doing things like this for their after school programs, Boys and Girl Clubs, sports teams and recreation leagues, summer camps, and Girl Scout troops all of the time. Why can't the alumnus of a student organization feel inspired to be the same way? Why not start an alumni chapter or division of your organization?

After graduation, the networking does not have to stop. The same way we studied together, we can support each other professionally. Let's just say, someone has a business, and another member becomes a lawyer, and another an accountant. What's wrong with the entrepreneur getting those two people to be his/her lawyer and accountant? If someone from your college organization becomes a doctor, what's wrong with you using his or her services? Or the person that becomes an accountant, why not get them to do your taxes? Why not send your child to the preschool started by one of your members? We should use the power of our networks, to help, support and promote each other's business and services. Why not go to someone that we associate with and trust? It's no different than people who were in the same fraternity, on the same team, or went to summer camp as youth together. All of the time and bonds built together should not be forsaken just because there was not a pledge process involved. There was a process and a struggle, and we went through it together, we grew up together.

Another question, why can't our general student organizations have legacies? Why don't we respect our organizations enough to even think that it's possible or a good idea? Think about this, people go to certain schools and join certain fraternities, sororities, social clubs, and teams because other members of their families did so. Why can't we have a legacy of student leadership, where people join student government because people in their family did it also? Why can't people walk onto a college campus and feel like there is an obligation of leadership and involvement? Why can't people join a general organization and have big shoes to fill, and high expectations, especially if you're in an activist, cultural, historical, umbrella or political organization? Why can't people enter college knowing they want to join a particular organization, because of their father, their older sister, their grandfather, their mentor was a part of an organization like that?

As an alumnus, you should want to lead by example, and as a student, you should want your alumni to lead and guide. Your alumni leave the university level to continue to open doors for you out in the world. When people leave your organization and graduate, your members should be beating down the door to get in the Alumni Association, so they can have a voice in making your organization relevant on another level and so they can have a voice in helping to improve the university. The Alumni Association can have an amazing amount of pull at some universities.

We often times underestimate what power we have as student organizations for change. We too often " overestimate what it takes and underestimate what we have"- **Lucson Joseph**.

Students at universities often have a litany of complaints and changes they'd like to see, yet often times they just verbalize the complaints but not act on them. They take for granted that their organizations can be the catalyst for change on many different levels. Whether that be; not liking the food options in the cafeteria or diversity issues on campus, wishing to start a recycling program to reduce waste on campus or concerns about the budgets allotted for student clubs and activities, conditions in the residence halls or a controversial bill to be voted on at city hall, increased tuition or statewide budget cuts. Regardless of the level (student government, university-wide, county, state, or national) student organization can, do, and will continue to have the power to change things. You not only have the power, you have the awesome responsibility to do and change things when you see things are wrong. Respect your abilities and force the rest of the world to respect your organization's capabilities also.

Getting In Our Own Way

The Pledge Process Problem: Greeks and Non Greeks Alike

In all my years of going to conferences and speaking with various organizations, the problem that consistently comes up, the most controversial and absolute hardest problem to fix is The Pledge Process Problem. The reason, because it's divisive, it's usually a long-standing and partly emotional problem, and the people who are the problem can't see or agree how they are dragging other organizations down. Neither can they see how it's their problem. It's also a situation where a majority of the club are ganging up and directly pointing fingers at the minority, and this small group of people is a scrutinized group already. In addition to this, a number of people that believe and may be vocal about the effects on the organization, those people will pledge and have a change of perspective and turn a blind eye to what's going on. There is also a reluctance to speak up and truly say what's on the minds of most, because often times the people addressing the problem possibly want to pledge themselves one day, and fear retribution. The problematic people are usually in denial about their role and have no interest in truly fixing it and they most certainly don't wish to be called to the carpet. The problem itself is that we have too many people using general student organizations as launching pads to Greek Life/ Pledge Organizations.

34

The hardest thing about the problem is there has to be an understanding of why/how it's an important issue. But this is also not something your organization can control or simply write a rule for. To fix it requires a cultural shift, some outside help, understanding, and participation from other organizations and governing bodies on both sides. This is also the problem that takes the longest to fix. Sometimes it won't happen within your time in the organization and sometimes it can never truly be fixed, just improved upon. Let's address the elephant in the room **The Pledge Process Problem**.

Let me make it plainly clear that The Pledge Process Problem is largely Greek, but it's not exclusively Greek Letter Organization members that are the problem. Any type of organization where people are required to go through an extra set of activities to be a part of the membership intake process, something more than just showing up, signing up and immediately getting involved, can and usually are the problem. No particular group is excluded, whether it's a women's group, men's group, business fraternity, law fraternity, societal group, fellowship, dance group or sports team. It's not that people pledge, but how they pledge and what happens to the general student organization immediately after they pledge, that makes them the problem for the average student organization.

Often times this is how it's done. A person will join a cultural, governmental, political, etc. organization, and because often times these types of organizations are struggling for membership and involvement, one can get involved at a high level relatively quickly. So the person will join, and be welcomed with open arms. Because, often times it's hard to get people to join the executive board or to be a committee head, and sometimes the organizations are kind of desperate. The executive board is often times ecstatic that someone/ anyone wants to be involved and help out. This individual will be embraced, cultivated and trained to be an effective leader for the foreseeable future. But this individual is only "putting in work", to appear involved on campus/ in the community so they can impress the group they need to impress. So they can be accepted to be a part of the pledge process. The deception is only part of the problem, it hurts the executive board or committee they're apart of because often times in the pledge process the individual starts to miss meetings, appointments, deadlines, events that they gave their word, bond and commitment that they would be apart of, because they're busy with the pledge process. This individual neglects their job, and now others are forced to pick up the slack. It is worse to have someone in a position not fulfilling his or her duties than it is to have the position vacant. If no one is in the position, at least if someone does ask about the job you can give it to him or her if they're interested. When no one is occupying the position, the executive board at least knows they will have to cover and split that positions work. However, when you're expecting someone to uphold their end of the bargain and they let you down, it's debilitating and frustrating.

But the true damage comes after the pledge process is complete. Usually, there is some type of induction ceremony, a probate show etc., where this individual will be introduced as being a member of your organization. Almost throwing it in your face and publicly shaming you as the fools they tricked. But most organizations and people in them will be right their proud and cheering them on as they join their new affiliation. What's really happening at this induction ceremony is that other people now know which organizations they can do the same thing too, because apparently your group doesn't mind and embraces this behavior. At some universities, it's almost encouraged to do so. Individuals will tell you which groups you can get over on. Yet, the worst of it comes after the induction, because too often and in too many organizations, after this individual gets their letters, jacket, paraphernalia, they will never or at best rarely, be active in your organization again. Suddenly, all of the training and knowledge they have gained will go to waste, because often times they will no longer be around to pass that knowledge and those skills on to a new generation. And it's disgraceful because most pledge organizations boast about their building up of leaders, and involvement for change. Yet at too many schools, you can hardly find pledged people in large numbers in student government, or leadership in any other club or activity. You can easily find whole chapters, where no one is involved in anything outside of pledge/ Greek life activities. You'll be lucky if they show up at general organization meetings and events, that their organization is not cosponsoring or they wish to make an announcement at. If they do, they'll often clique up with other pledged people, and even if they come to an event some will only socialize with other pledged people.

I can hear the arguments now, that it's easier to become one than to be one, and that's true. However, many are not taught to balance their new affiliations and their prior commitments. Which is a shame, because many of their prophytes found a way to do just that. Many feel once inducted to these new affiliations that nothing else matters, and all of their loyalty and time is to be with the new love of their life. Forgetting that the general student organization was their first family and first purpose. The general student organization built them up and legitimized them, but they treat it now as if it's an option rather than a priority.

One of my mentors once scolded a group of new pledges that, "All of your friends [have not pledged], and everybody that [has pledged] is not your friend, you are not better than anyone, so don't act like you can't socialize and be a part of things like everyone else." You expand your networks and friendships, not make them exclusive.

Across this nation, you can easily find student organizations where the majority, if not the entire leadership structure is pledging. But sadly it's rare to find an organization where the majority of the leadership structure has already pledged. The general student organization at this stage is a façade, a farm, and filter system for pledges and prospects. The general student organization has been relegated to minor league status on many campuses. Think about it, in many cases, we speak of people that have pledged in past tense form. "They used to be a part of this organization", "They once were very involved", "We haven't seen them since they pledged, they used to be a leader." So the message that is sent is, it's okay to give your all to the pledge group, but only 10, 25, 50% or whatever you can spare of effort to the general student org. There is an implied message that you only have to be involved, only have to be a leader prior to pledging. That speaks to commitment because truly committed people understand commitment, love, respect, and consistency across the board in all of their doings.

Not all people that pledge are deceitful, uncommitted, irresponsible, and untrustworthy that abandon their previous organization. Some people do a wonderful job of balancing their commitments and passion for their general organization while pledging. But it's a double-edged sword, and just as detrimental. Because for every person that pledges in this "responsible" manner, 9 or 10 will mess it up, trying to attempt it. The reality is you've now opened the door for others that may wish to pledge, to believe that it's okay to pledge while on an executive board. Once it's been done, no matter how carefully, how do you tell someone else that they can't do the same thing without looking like a hypocrite?

The individual that pledges instantly gets a large audience, and popularity and people will copycat their moves into the new affiliation, good or bad. Over the long haul, your organization suffers because your best-trained, best-educated, best-equipped, most prepared leaders are taking their knowledge, popularity, and influence away from your organization. Some of your elite members and what should be the future of your organization are now subtracted, so who does that leave to oversee the organization? The general organization is now left in the hands of the unprepared, untrained, uninvolved, unmotivated and uneducated. People that are ill trained and ill equipped. Do you really expect prosperity?

It truly is a shame that it often ends up like this, because most pledge organizations and general organizations with a purpose, often have similar or the same purposes and principles. And many times a person from the general organization was influential in starting a chapter of the pledge process or vice versa. Given these points, the disconnect between the two worlds is baffling

So how do you combat The Pledge Process Problem?

First and foremost your organization has to start from within. In many student organizations, there used to be a time-honored and an unwritten rule (**The Knowledge Problem**) that it was frowned upon to pledge, while on an executive board, because no matter how you did it would always look as if you used the general organization to get your letters or status, etc. And, because the pledge process requires so much time and attention you wouldn't be able to complete your duties, so it was out of respect to other organizations. Hence student groups have to share, teach and frown upon this practice and not be accepting of it.

Secondly, we have to address offending organizations individually and as groups. Meaning it may be necessary to address their councils or umbrella organizations because you can't do it by yourself, you likely can't write rules that prohibit this type of pledging. But find out from your student government and student affairs if that's a rule that can be written in. Start the discussion. Address your concerns on all levels, speak to the chapter and it's leaders, get the Student Affairs, Greek Affairs, get advisors of the offending organizations involved to look for solutions. Encourage members that if they wish to take a sabbatical or step down and pledge its alright, or do it over the summer, anything just not while executive board or committee members, and to stay active after pledging. There has to be a culture shift. Do not be afraid to address the pledge organizations directly, they're students also, not the mafia. The problem will never go away or get better if it's just allowed to continue on. The problem will fester and resentment will form. Pledged members have to be held to a higher standard because they have set a higher standard for themselves. Let's all hold them to that higher standard and expectation. A process where more work is put in after the pledge process, than work put in to begin it. After you pledge there should be a rebirth of sorts. An individuals legacy is what they do after they pledge, everything before is water under the bridge. The stakes are raised tremendously.

In an ideal situation, pledge organizations will work with general student organizations. When individual come to their interest meetings they'll let them know that it's frowned upon to pledge in that manner, that they grow and cultivate leaders and that it's frowned upon to not be active after pledging, so the message will be communicated multiple times and reinforced from both sides, causing less tension. Also, ideally when individuals go to interest meeting with their resume and claim to be a part of said general organizations, the organizations they are trying to pledge with would do their due diligence and check with other organizations to see if and to what extent they are involved. People should not be allowed to misrepresent their self or another organization, to get involved in another. It's so fraudulent and disingenuous. As a leader I routinely had pledge masters contact me after interest meetings to find out if certain people were really a part of my organization or a certain committee, and if so how active. That's mutual respect.

Pledge organizations already know this is a problem. It's well documented that pledge organizations have problems too; despite having knowledge, knowing their history, and having well-documented legacies in their own organization. At the national level, they spend a lot of time discussing intake process, participation levels and the quality of members they take in. The discussion needs to be had that after pledging, members don't have to choose sides, they can operate in both worlds. Perhaps they need to be trained to operate in both or explained as to why it's important to operate in both, because when a member of a pledge organization is forced to choose between the two, hands down the pledge organization wins because they earned that distinction, paid for that distinction and they worked for that distinction. The general organization is given as opposed to earned, which makes it of less value in some people eyes.

Which connects us back to **The Respect Problem**, and leads us into the **Participation Problem**.

The Participation Problem

Students are often told to join an organization and to get involved on campus. More importantly than join, they need to be encouraged to get engaged and to participate in the organization.

In too many of our organizations, we have 20% of people doing 80% of the work. We have people that are in, but not a part of the organization. We have people that are interested when it's convenient or beneficial for them, but they're not committed to the organization. They are in, but they're inactive and inactive people are useless to an organization. Inactive people will keep your organization from growing and prospering and will ensure you stay stagnant.

Most problems, issues, gripes, and complaints in an organization can usually be traced to the complainer's lack of participation. The first thing that needs to be addressed in most organizations is that it's your organization, not just the executive boards. Your organization and what happens to it is everyone's responsibility. When an organization complains to me about their student government, the first question I ask is how many people does the club have actively participating in student government? There is a saying in politics that "either you're at the table or you're on the menu."

If you want to improve your organization and address any complaints or attempts to make it better, the first thing that needs to be asked is an individual question. What do you do for the organization? Every single member of the organization needs to have a job, and contribute something. You can and should participate in various degrees with your time, your talent and your treasure. Your time is how do you make yourself available for the organization, so you can be of use and help out? Your talent, what is that you do well and can contribute? Your treasure can be a number of things; it may be you contributing your fair expected share for club dues and additional offerings if you have it to give. Your treasure can consist of you sponsoring someone else in the club that is less fortunate. If someone can't afford to pay their dues or other expenses, and you feel compelled and can help them, do so. If you can afford to donate more than the minimum for dues, do so.

 Your treasure could also be your connections in the community or your influence on the campus. Your treasure might be knowledge, experiences, and expertise you bring to a situation. So what is it that everyone does, besides show up to meetings, get the free t-shirts, eat the food and complain about how things could be better, or what should have been done? How much do you /they contribute to the success and failure of the organization? Do you live up to the legacy of the organization or are you just living off of it? Everyone complains and points fingers when something is wrong, but everyone wants to share in the credit when things go right.

What is it that you are doing for your organization? Are you on a committee? Are you in Student Government for this organization, looking out for issues that might affect them? Are you on some type of Council of Student Organizations assuring we get a fair shake when it comes to credibility and funding, or that rules are implemented justly? Are you on the finance committee? Are you on the events planning committee? Are you on the marketing team, helping to advertise the events and promote the club? Do you set up events or break down and clean up afterward? Are you on hospitality for welcoming and taking care of guest and performers? What is it that you do? What do you do more than just show up? What do you do more than just attend the event? How are you an asset to the group, rather than a liability?

Everyone in your organization should have a job, everyone has to contribute something, and there should not be a member who does not have a task. In too many organizations we have an abundance of people that do nothing and are involved in nothing. Everyone should buy into the idea that the organization is a little bit better and a little bit stronger or a little bit worse and a little bit weaker because of him or her. Each individual's effort matters and benefits the group. Everyone has to take ownership of the organization. Everyone has to share in both the successes and the failures.

Every single person has to understand that the organization can have an infinite amount of leaders. You can be a good or bad leader; a good or bad influence from any position within the organization, you don't have to be appointed or elected to be a leader/influential. It cannot be expected nor proven to be true, that the executive board and committee heads will do all the work and nothing is expected or required from anyone else. If that is the practice, you will set your organizations up for current and future leadership burnout. Leadership burnout or battle fatigue is when you get sick and tired of being the only one trying to make a difference. It's when you lose your enthusiasm and desire to be involved. You get disheartened with seemingly fighting the good fight aloneis your become displeased being the only one willing to step up and step out. Fed up seeming like the only one who cares and not being appreciated or helped. In fact, it needs to be ingrained in everyone that it is not the advisor's, president's or executive board's job to do everyone else's task, but to help everyone do their jobs better and more effectively. Everyone has to be actively committed to making the organization better, carrying out the organization's mission and improving experiences for each member. For organizational success it must be understood that commitment is an obligation, not an option; it's a daily attitude.

In order to get everyone involved, in your organization three things have to occur: 1. The long-term benefits must be shown. 2. The culture has to be created and promoted. 3. The benefits of the organization have to be merit based.

1. **The long-term benefits** of being involved in an organization are seldom expressed or used to convince people to be involved. The first thing that has to be done is to remove all the excuses for why one can't or doesn't want to be involved. It's usually hardest to get people to join student government or some type of legislative body, and the excuses usually thrown around the most are, "I don't have time", "I don't want to deal with the drama and aggravation" or " I don't like those kinds of people".

Make it clear to these individuals that in life you will never have enough time, you make time to do or be apart of things that are important to you. College is a training ground, a dress rehearsal for real life experiences. A lot of college students seem to believe that after college you'll have more time to do the things you want and need to do, that things are impossible in college because you have to go to class, work, and study, have family duties, etc. Well contrary to popular belief, these things you experience in undergrad are constants, not variables, and they take up more of your time after college, leaving you with even less time. If these things are allowed to be excuses as an undergrad; you'll never have time to be involved, it'll never be the right time. College involvement teaches you to effectively manage your time for your obligations and other interests. Of course, you are at school for an education and to graduate, but that is not an excuse to do nothing beyond that. There is nothing wrong with doing some productive socializing and gaining some rewarding experiences. People have to realize two things:

1.   Your circumstances are not unique, the people that are involved in the organization, have families, they have to study, work etc. also.
2.   You're not the first person to go through this, leaders and involved people before you had to graduate and study also.

Lack of time is not an excuse because once you graduate, instead of class, it's your job or career, and sometimes you still have class if you're working on your masters or a specialist degree. You still have to study; you still have family, church etc. Instead of going to club meetings it'll be parent-teacher association, home owners association, union meetings, it's city meetings etc., time is never convenient you never get much of it. You either make time for things important to you or you make excuses. The things you learn from being involved in college and the schedule you keep don't change after college. The way that a Student Government Meeting runs is very similar to the way a city commission meeting runs. The world is a big student government. If you learn to write and vote on a bill in student government, you can technically do the same in the Halls of Congress, because the process is the same. It's a little more intense and the ramifications are bigger, but basically the same. Roberts Rule of Order is used at most official meetings, and even by some companies in the boardroom.

As for the excuses, "I don't want to deal with the drama and aggravation" or " I don't like those kinds of people", let it be known those issues don't change either. Drama, politics, and aggravation happen on all levels of life, leadership, involvement and government. The back and forth banter, negotiations and "red tape" are part of any form of involvement and the people that make being involved so difficult, they don't stop being involved once they graduate. The people that make things difficult go on to be leaders in bigger arenas that matter way more than affecting your clubs policy or budget. The people that make things difficult they become; head of your home owners association, they are leaders of workers unions, they become your city council members, county commissioners, the heads of your school boards, where now they have real power and can affect real things. They can now affect where you live, how you live, your pension, where your child goes to school and their future. Thus you can either run from and avoid these types of people and be told what to do, or you can have a voice in the process and confront them, and bring others ideas to the table. As Martin Luther King stated, "It's always the right time, to do the right thing."

Telling people what they can do to contribute to the organization 2.**creates the culture**. Most people want to help and be involved; they just don't know how what they are doing actually helps, and how to get involved or where to start. So the leadership needs to inform the members of which committees are available (if there are any), what each one does, and that everybody needs to be a part of, remain active and involved in at least one, and then do committee sign-ups. I say at least one because some are willing to do more, and that should be encouraged, all committees are not always active at the same point in time, and some committees have special times or seasons when they are in use. The goal is to ensure that everyone has a chance to become and remains involved.

When I was a leader of an organization we treated joining a committee as if you were joining the church. We'd welcome you to the organization, and then ask which committee you wanted to join? If you didn't know, that was fine. We'd give you a pamphlet with all of the committees and their responsibilities on them and at the next meeting, I would expect for you to have made a decision. If you choose not to pick a committee I can assign you to one, but I rather give you the choice, because you are more likely to have interest and be passionate about your choice. If they couldn't choose, then as a leader you have to be creative in getting them involved. Sometimes people really don't know what to be a part of. If you have to assign someone a committee, here are two ways that worked best for me, get them involved based on their major or based on their interest and sell them the benefits of it.

For example, I used to have a young man that used to sit in the front row of all meetings, and the whole time he'd draw, and doodle, all over the agenda. So I asked him to be a part of the marketing committee and design the flyers, the calendar, pamphlets etc. We had a very tech savvy individual, so he designed our website and was the webmaster. We had a young man in the organization that was a party promoter, so he was asked to be a part of marketing team; he had the experience and he knew how to advertise to college students. He used to have this little slogan that he was about, "getting bodies in the building and putting asses in seats." Well excellent, because when we had a meeting, or an event that's exactly what I want and need "bodies in the building and asses in seats", so please help me accomplish that.

Had a young lady that had a very bubbly, very warm personality. She always made people feel welcome, so I asked her to head up the hospitality committee. Because if we had a performer coming, the first thing I wished was for them to feel welcomed and appreciated, and I wanted someone that was willing to accommodate the guest. Keep them company, make sure the amenities they need are accessible, is the room to their expectation, do they need any additional assistance?

I had a young lady that was an accounting major, so I definitely asked her to be on the finance committee and eventually, she became the treasurer. She was able to use her position as experience for her future career. Where else between age 18-22 was she going to get experience managing and writing a six-figure budget, or coming up with ideas to fundraise if needed?

People that were interested in fashion, we're encouraged to join the marketing team and help design t-shirts. If you were interested in event planning or interior decorating, be a part of the planning committee so you would have input on the decoration for an event or the theme of the banquet. I had a group of skeptics and critics, no matter what event we would do it was never good enough for them. They would always have a complaint about; the number of people that attended, the food that was served, what should have been done; and in response, we created a committee to put that criticism to productive use. They were the evaluation committee. They'd have evaluations at each event and they'd work with the other committees, so we'd know why the event went a particular way, was it promoted enough, did we have the correct budget, was there another event happening at the same time, causing a conflict? They were basically research and development of the organization.

We used to also make it clear that everybody in the organization was a part of the marketing committee and responsible for promoting an event.

There should never be a point in time where people don't know about an event. Any and everybody can put up flyers, actually the more of us the better, and the quicker it will go. Everybody can post a social media message about the event, we can all personally invite people, and if you were in other organizations you can go up in open forum and remind them and invite them to the event. Any and everyone can grab some quarter flyers and pass them out. Anyone can be in charge of setting up the club's table in one of the gathering spots or for a club fest on campus and pass out flyers, remind or invite people to a meeting, or sign people up for the organization. If your school has a Freshman Move-In Day for on-campus residents, organize as many people from your club as possible to volunteer for this event. Use this as an opportunity to strike up a conversation as you are assisting them in getting settled in. Offer them a flyer, and invite them to an event. You've just killed two birds with one stone; you've recruited and marketed an upcoming event.

The marketing team can take over all forms of media. Someone can make an announcement on the campus radio station, another can get the event posted on the university website, get the event advertised in the campus paper and have them cover the event, get the event put on local radio and local newspapers websites (it's usually free, especially if they have a community page, and you may get some coverage), and advertise at other schools in the local area. If you have a student-run television channel make a commercial and get them to film the event. Find out what's the price and process of getting an event placed on the on campus billboards or video boards. What's the process of getting an event announced at a sporting event or other large events?

On the day of the event, how do we get ground signs that point the direction to an event? Everybody can do and should do something.

Remember most people won't knock down your door asking for work, yet most people want to be involved but they don't know how.
Sometimes your organization can be too big, or too cliquish, and leaders can be intimidating, to the point that no one wants to approach us. Interact with people; don't force them to come to you. Your job is to figure out how to get them involved

Another recommendation, the executive board should always have an open door policy. If a member wants to see certain documentation, let them know they are welcome. Inform members, when executive board meetings are and if they wish to attend they can. General members attending an executive board meeting, promotes transparency in the organization, and it gives the opportunity for every voice and every idea to be heard and considered before decisions are made.

If everybody does his or her part it won't be that hard or take up too much of anybody's time. There is an old African proverb that says, "Many hands, make for light work." The organization is a machine; it's a body, a living organism. It's not just an organization; if one part is not working correctly it places unnecessary stress on other parts. It doesn't matter if you've been in the organization 5 minutes or 5 years, everybody has an important role.

The third part is **merit based**.

There are a number of ways people take advantage of our organizations. The reason they do so is because they know that there aren't any repercussions because it often goes unpunished and unchecked. The lack of consequences for being inactive or inconsistent in organizations is very inviting to people who don't really wish to do anything, and extremely discouraging for committed members, because often times the benefits and reward are exactly the same. It often doesn't matter if you've been consistent all year long, been active in a committee, attended meetings, events, and functions. A person who has been none of this will get the exact same benefits and can buck the system, and still have influence within the organization. They can run for office and become leadership, they can obtain a recommendation letter as if they were a model member, they have our support, have an untarnished reputation, they get awards at our banquets and go to trips and conferences, all while doing nothing for the organization. The organization gives them everything and in return, they give it nothing.

We often look to see if they show up to an event and overlook those that are consistently there. Think about this, if you can get all of the benefits for doing nothing, why would you ever want to actually sacrifice, work and put effort into being in the organization? Your effort and work will just go unnoticed and unappreciated anyway. The squeaky wheel may get the oil, but the proper functioning wheels deserve the tire shine. We often times as leader overlook those that are doing right and focus on those that are not. We often times don't give recognition or enough appreciation to those that are actively following and working with us. Yet when the inconsistent ones do the slightest thing, we shower them with praise and are proud of them for doing what they should be doing, rather than giving that attention to those that go above and beyond.

How does this become a problem and how do we combat it?
Anytime people don't have to earn their rewards, a sense of entitlement forms. And when people are rewarded for

any sliver of effort, and it is treated the same as maximum effort, it takes away any incentive to do more or do better. Why be on the front lines if you can be on the sidelines and get the same perks. As sad as it may be we have to give incentive, bonuses, and rewards to our members that our distinguished and exemplary.

It may seem weird but it's the norm everywhere else in life, we reward positive performance. In grade school we reward, perfect attendance, we reward good grades by having assemblies and recognizing those that made the honor roll. If you keep that up when you graduate, you receive offers to good schools and programs, scholarships, grants, fellowships and at graduation you have all kinds of honors and stoles and chords. In sports, benchmarks and milestones are rewarded with bonuses, all-star game appearances, all league teams, special awards and other honors. In your career, you may get recognition, corner offices, raises, promotions, extra vacation time, benefits packages. There are things you get for doing the bare minimum, for just being apart and just showing up and then there are other things you have to earn; everybody has the same opportunity to access these things but not all will, because maybe you have a certain amount of time credited, or meet a quota.

Usually, at a job, you have to be on probation 90-180 days or more before you have access to benefits, and job security. So why can't we take these examples and apply them to our student organizations? Once again I'll remind you, we should think of our student organizations as a business because we are training and producing leaders. The first thing we should be doing is taking attendance. Take attendance at every meeting, event, and function.

Have a sign-up sheet and make sure that everything means something and everything counts for something. Social events may count one way and possibly cultural, community service, educational events count for more, but everything has to be recorded and be paid attention to. If the club has membership dues, you have to be paid in full in order to vote, travel, etc., but everything counts for something.

You can take those attendance records and use them for multiple things. Analyze them see what kind of events are best attended, and the deeper the analysis the better. See who attends what kinds of events. Pay attention to trends, if someone has stop attending; contact them to find out if they are ok. Perhaps they're just busy, maybe they're having a family circumstance, or they're no longer interested, but they'll appreciate you checking on them. That personal touch is the family atmosphere. It's business but we're still a family.

 Now on a business side, you can use those attendance records for other things, such as fairly deciding who is your member of the year or executive board member of the year, or worthy of special recognition at the end of the award banquet? Set some rigid standards and various accomplishment marks.

For instance, in one of my organizations we used to have a gold pin, it was something you earned and treasured, not everyone had it and you couldn't buy it. People were proud to have that pin, people wanted to get that pin. For continued excellent service in your college career in the club, we had a graduation stole for you. Once again, not everybody got one, and you couldn't purchase it, you had to earn it. A message was being sent, that you get what you earn. You get out of this organization what you put into it. When I was a leader, I'd implement a percentage of events or amount of points a person would have to reach in order to even be considered to go on an out of town trip or a conference. I did that because when it comes to conferences people often buck the system. They'll be too

busy or not interested all year long and then magically
they had all the time in the world when it's time for the
conference, suddenly they can get time off from work, and
studying was no longer important. They'll get to go to a
conference and usually for the wrong reasons because
they'll treat conference as a party road trip, not a
business trip, but they'll get to go because they have the
money.

When I was a leader, a conference was a privilege, not a
birthright; you had to earn this opportunity with your
consistency. When we went to a conference, I wanted
people that were going to learn, pay attention and not
embarrass the organization by playing around. If we went
to a conference we often had to have an epic battle with
the student government to get the money, so I wasn't
going to waste the organization's fight or the money by
taking people who didn't deserve it or were a risk. You
couldn't just show up with money and go, you had to
earn it. You can go, but not on our dime. If you still
wanted to go to conference you could pay your own hotel
and registration, but you were not going to get over on the
student government or my organization. It showed
responsibility to the student government and school
administration, by having a standard like that it showed
we were about business, not games.

The same way there was equal opportunity in the
organization, there was and always should be equal
consequences. Just because you were appointed or an
elected member did not mean you automatically received
perks or the chance to go to a conference, leaders had to
earn everything also. You cannot expect from the pews
what you don't show from the pulpit. In fact, the
standard was actually higher for leaders, leaders should
always be held to a higher standard, and the
consequences were also. If you couldn't make a certain
percentage of meetings and events, then you could and

should be stripped of your title, and removed from office, and don't even think you're in consideration for an outing or a perk. And that goes for anyone in a profile position including your pageant and homecoming titles of Mr. & Ms. (insert Organization name). If you can't hold up the standard, then it can be taken from you. If you can't meet the requirements, you can't be rewarded the benefits. So now the culture has been changed. It's not who wants to go to, or is interested in going, it's who is eligible to attend the conference based on participation and attendance records and rather you were paid in full on your club dues by the established deadline. Because everyone is interested, but who has earned it, is a totally different story. Award, rewards, benefits and titles, are performance based perks.

We found ways to even make people respect our time and types of event. You wish to go to conference or a field trip, great! we operate on a first ready, first come, first serve basis. You need to have all of your required paperwork and payments in on time. If you showed up on time to an event or meeting you were allowed to sit wherever you wanted, but if you came late, you were ushered to a seat, usually in the front. Eventually, people learned to be on time. The only type of time we acknowledge and respect is on time. We taught people to respect the type of events we had, by not advertising food or giveaways, or when they would happen. If we had food, we would serve it at various moments and at various events, no one knew when to expect food and when not to, unless it was obvious like a dinner or a barbecue, but sometimes the food would be served as you walked in, sometimes we'd have intermission and it would be served then, and sometimes it would be at the end. Sometimes we'd serve the food, sometimes it'd be buffet style, sometimes a whole meal, sometimes a few appetizers, regardless it'd only be served once and we didn't save plates, you had to be there or you missed out. Consequently, people learned to come for the actual event not for the food. The same thing with giveaways and door prizes, you were not going to be rewarded with food and gifts, for showing up late and disrupting what was in progress or not showing at all, when others not only came but also were on time and maybe helped out.

One last thing, once or twice per semester, perform evaluations for your organization. Presidents should evaluate your executive board members, as a group and individually. Then, allow the executive board to evaluate you and the job you're doing. Have the committee heads evaluate each of their committee members, and the committee members evaluate the committee head. Have the membership evaluate the executive board as a whole and have the advisor evaluate the executive board and vice versa. By doing evaluations, it reinforces that everyone is being watched by each other, and holds everyone accountable to each other and the organization. The evaluation shows everyone what he or she is doing positively, what he or she needs to improve on and what's expected of him or her. Evaluations let everyone know that their participation and involvement is being noticed. At the end of the year, you can use the evaluations to possibly give a most improved award or to figure out who was most consistent all year long if you have a member of the year.

There are a myriad of ways you can reward and restrict people. Have a member of the month. If you order items for giveaways, order some with the intention of them being earned, so maybe everyone gets a t-shirt, but you have to earn the button up or polo shirt. Everyone may get the ink pen and pencil, but you have to earn the binder with the club's logo on it. Everyone may get the lanyard, but you earn the pin.

Before I would agree to write a recommendation letter for anything, I would have the organization's secretary pull up attendance and participation records.

These actions lead back to respect for the organization, it rewards and encourages participation, but proper and disciplined participation. You don't get the same perks for doing nothing, as someone that has been giving their all. That's not fair, balanced, equal, respectable or realistic. You get out of the organization what you put into it. You respect the organizations time and events, and it will respect and reward your time, work and effort.

The Cooperation Problem

The most troubling problem organizations have today is a huge cooperation problem. Too many organizations wish to be the only show in town and attempt to be all things to all people. No matter how big or small your purpose, it's important that you work with other organizations rather than insulate yourself. Your organization cannot do it all and you cannot do it by yourself, neither should you try. On most campuses and just in general there are too many organizations having unnecessary rivalries, with other organizations that they should be allies with. Having beef between organizations is not good for anybody. This practice is distracting, and it is counterproductive.

There is nothing wrong with friendly, healthy competition, but rivalries lead to hostilities and can be destructive. Competition makes you better and it breed's healthy respect. There's nothing wrong with having a healthy respect for what another organization does, but be competitive not combative. There is nothing wrong with a good will athletic or academic competition against another organization, or a race to see who can raise the most money for a good cause. Good will events for a good cause foster cooperation. But, when there is no cooperation, there is a lack of organization, a lack of unity and a lack of strength.

On too many campuses, there exist a huge gulf between organizations, especially similar organizations that keep them from working together. The division and confusion keep them all struggling.

When it comes to cooperation, too many organizations don't know how to work with or around other university-wide, and this leads to competition for members, budgets, event attendance, and other resources. All which could be avoided if organizations would communicate with each other and work with each other.

Many organizations end up working against themselves, by not working with or consulting with other organizations both at their school and off campus. Too many organizations operate as if they exist in a vacuum. But in actuality, if you pay attention at most schools, you'll find out that there are too many organizations attempting to do the same thing and that the pathways are crowded. First and foremost because most clubs and organizations do not know how to play their position, and stay in their lane. Meaning, they lack their own original creative ideas and identity. Instead, they will copy other club's and organization's events and ideas, in an attempt to manufacture another group's experience. Which takes us all the way back to **The Knowledge Problem**. Because people don't know what kind of organization they have, they treat leadership like a derby rather than a race. In a derby, you're allowed to be all over the place, but in a race, you have an assigned lane. Not saying your organization should never do anything outside of it's stated purpose or type, but be consistent and original, know when to yield to other organizations and not step on their toes.

This derby mentality often becomes an issue when new organizations are formed. Often times, new organizations are formed because one of the older organizations has changed and are not living up to what they are supposed to be. But rather than try to fix the old organizations, we further separate and usually, the newer organizations often attempt to replace or be like another organization. They do the same kind of events; have similar audience and purposes with very minute variations.

But by not working together what ends up happening is a weakening of all the organizations and never being able to fulfill their Multi-Cultural, because what organizations often fail to realize is that they are usually pulling from the same pool of resources (money, influence, and people) and that pool is more often than not, shrinking rather than growing, and a lot more could be accomplished and lot more success had if organizations learned to pool resources and help each other out. Especially, when you have a smaller organization, there is an umbrella organization that can bring multiple organization together, there is a greater cause or just for the sake of having harmonious mutually beneficial relationships.

Most Organizations would greatly benefit if they approached cooperation in these four ways

1.   Learn to not work against yourself (plan around your competition)
2.   Learn to consolidate power
3.   Learn to get the community involved (Outside of campus)
4.   Learn to work a conference

1.   **Learn to not work against yourself** – When you're planning an event or activity, the two words that will serve you well are, communication and research. There is nothing worse as a student than having five or six events going on one night, then absolutely no events the next night. And there is nothing worse as a student leader than to have an event planned and know that half of your

target audience is going to be at another event going on at the same time. Events take a lot of time, effort and money to plan. So, give yourself, organization, and event the best chance for success by doing your best to not have to compete against another similar or big event if possible.

It goes back to thinking of our organization in terms of business. Something as simple as the date of your event can make or break it. In the event planning world, regardless of whether, it's a movie, televisions premiere, album release, award show, or championship fight. The first thing they want to assure is that they pick a day that does not hurt the chances of success. You will never see a championship fight on the same night as the Super Bowl. The window of that time the Super Bowl is on, other channels will not be airing their most important or popular shows, they may try to get views before the game and possibly after. Treat your organization and events the same way. An age-old saying applies to planning events, "if you fail to plan, you plan to fail."

When you plan your events sit down with a calendar, and plug in all the known events, as you know them to happen. First, account for big popular events, possible football games, basketball games, comedy shows, coffee houses, etc., big popular events that you don't want to have to compete against. Next, account for other similar organizations known meeting times, traditional events and frequently scheduled events. Then if you want to use that day still, find a way to have your event start and end either before the regularly scheduled event or directly after it. If it's after, you can go to the meeting for example and announce your event in open form, or pass out flyers directing people to your event. You don't want to split your audience if it's not necessary. When students are given too many choices, what usually will happen is after a while they'll opt out of all choices because they don't want to pick a side.

When you're planning events, keep other organizations with similar audiences, interest, purposes, or similar cultural/social ties informed of your plans so that they don't plan an even on top of you. By doing this you have the opportunity to attend other organizations events and to invite other organizations to your events.

By communicating with other organizations you possess the potential to do more co-sponsorships. Co-sponsorship's give you the opportunity to expand your audience, do bigger events and share the responsibility. This is something especially important to consider if you have a small organization, a small budget or if there are a number of the same events happening on your campus.

Instead of five different gospel shows, or six different fashion shows, or multiple game nights and poetry nights/talent shows that are only fairly attended, why not combine forces and do a big event together. Besides expanding your organization's networking opportunity and fostering new relationships, co- sponsorship's make the event bigger and expands your access to a larger audience. It gives you more manpower to work with and advertise the event; it allows you to share in the responsibility and it increases the amount of money you have to spend on the event.

But also, instead of having a multitude of events on one night, we can spread them out and there will always be something to do on campus.

Work with as many organizations as possible, whenever possible, it will open up so many opportunities for you. Co-sponsorships are about building relationships and strong alliances and fostering respect among organizations. So don't just attempt to cosponsor an event only when you have a problem or it's a mutual interest. Sometimes offer or accept an event where your interest is not the primary reason for seeking it. It's not about your event or having competition, but you'd just like to work with another organization you respect. Do an event with an organization outside of your normal audience, culture, and purpose. Try to broaden your audience and spread the word, try to get the athletes involved and to participate in your club. Look for ways to get graduate students involved. Do an event with some people that don't look like you or believe like you. As much as you want to spread your cause, culture, or interest, it's equally important to be accepting of other group's causes, culture, events, and interest, and be willing to attend and help with their events also. The things you have in common are way more than your differences, so focus on those things, and build events around that. By doing things like this you not only build respect and willing partners, but you expand the experiences and horizons of your members by exposing them to new things.

2.**Learn to Consolidate Power** – There are certain times, events and initiatives that require a coordinated effort from numerous organizations working in concert in order to pull off or improve something. When these situations arise, it's important for organizations to know how to step back and play a role without being in charge, and let one specific organization lead the effort. Several factors can determine who leads; it could be **manpower**, where the largest organization leads the effort. **Money**, where the organization that has the largest budget or is contributing the most funds is in charge. **Capability**, the organization with the expertise, experience or structure leads the effort. Or **interest**, the organization that came up with the idea, or it's their primary issue/cause/celebration/tradition. It's usually a good

opportunity for an umbrella organization, to unite
everyone and lead, and if one exists, it's recommended.

 When dealing with multiple groups/ multiple executive
boards, it's important everyone is in the know and
understands their role, everyone is constantly kept in the
loop and that each group's terms are agreed upon, laid
out and clear from the beginning. When operating in
large-scale cooperation mode, think in terms of a fist. The
fist represents all of us as one unit, and each group
represents a finger.

Diversity and multiculturalism is a big issue at most
campuses and large-scale cooperation is one of the best
ways to achieve those types of goals. For instance, my
organizations would handle working together on Black
History Month. Since the Black Student Union was the
umbrella organization they would call a meeting with all
of the groups. At the
meeting would be the Caribbean Student Association and
the National Pan-Hellenic Council
(Black Greek Letter Organizations), both umbrella
organizations in their own right.
The Haitian Student Organization, NAACP, Students
United for Africa, the National Society of Black Engineers,
the Latin American Students Organization because they
are culturally and historically tied to African Americans,
the Multi Cultural Greek Council etc., etc., Also in
attendance we'd invite the Office of Multicultural Affairs,
International Affair, the History Department, the English
Department and the Office of Housing and Residential
Life, because those departments would often throw Black
History events also.

Once everybody was in the room we began to throw out
ideas on what types of events we had planned and would
like to see for Black History Month. We'd ask for at least
one event to be hosted by each group. So an event from

the Caribbean perspective, an event from the Haitian perspective, the Hispanic perspective, NAACP would give us a historic event, African students group would give us the perspective of Black History Month from students born and raised in Africa. The National Society of Black Engineers would give us an event around the accomplishments of black people in science and technology, the business fraternity may have an event around black business history. We'd ask for one event from each Black Greek Letter Organization and one from them as the unified National Pan-Hellenic Council.

Then we'd do the same with the various departments and offices (Multicultural Affairs, International Affairs, The Art Galleries, etc.). Then we'd begin to place these events on a calendar to make sure none of them conflicted with each other. Now the big-budget organizations can pool their resources and attempt to go after a big name national speaker or throw some other grand event. We can plan a black faculty/staff meet and greet social. Now that everything is organized, even if we have multiple events on one day none are clashing. The whole months events are on one calendar and one flyer for students to see, and there is plenty to do and experience that month. By doing this, the events that the departments and offices would throw are now advertised side by side with student events and as a result are much better attended. Having the Office of Housing and Residential Life on Board is a huge accomplishment, because they often times have events you have to compete with, but they are also looking for programming for their residents. And by having them on board they can advertise to non-residents and expand their audience, and now rather than just having the Resident Assistants you personally know advertise an event, you now have the whole staff in partnership advertising an event or cultural month.

We would reproduce this exact routine for every cultural Month, Hispanic Heritage Month, Jewish History Month, Native American Heritage, and Women's History Month etc. The organizations would change and the groups and offices, but the process remained the same. And we'd continue to expand. We'd ask the program board/ activities board if for the monthly comedy show and coffee house if they could book an act that reflected that month's theme/culture. We'd check with the student body president and governor of the campus and see if they had any money in their special projects account they'd like to contribute. Now the whole school is involved and groups are seeking us out to find a way to get involved, the campus is becoming unified.

By sharing our plans, hopes and expectations for these cultural months, we are able to see if we can meet or exceed those expectations. If not we could do the best we could and strategize on how we could do better to meet full expectations for the next month or next year. By collaborating you're able to do a lot more, with significantly less.

This process could be used for various causes. You could collaborate on a large-scale community service event. If you get a number of community service organizations and maybe some community service fraternities and sororities, then take a large group of people to do a project or have a philanthropic effort. Or what if you do a beach cleanup, and involve the environmental club, Marine Biology Department, and the Urban Planning department and associated clubs. Think of how powerful that image is publicly, a number of organizations from said school/university; got together for this cause, there truly is strength in numbers. The collaboration allows multiple people to get to network and accomplish together, and these may be people who otherwise would have no other reason to be around each other. Now we all get the credit, the school looks great, and individuals have the chance to be there representing multiple organizations. A person may have the opportunity to represent and spend time with their club and their fraternity/sorority families on one project at the same time, all while accomplishing something worthwhile and not have to choose a side.

Another example the Caribbean students would have an annual fashion show. Several different cultures, African, Asian, and Hispanic represent the Caribbean. So when planning the fashion show, we'd contact the Latin American Student organizations, Asian Student groups and the modeling troupe on campus to participate in the fashion show. Ideally, the fashion and entertainment would represent the influences of each culture, so the whole Caribbean was represented.

The consolidation process was also used on a political scale to make changes at our school. When student government elections happened, we'd get all the multicultural organizations together, and tell them to get at least two representatives to run for SG. When election time came around, we'd send out an email with the names of every individual that was in our co-op regardless what ticket they ran with. Once elected, we'd have people on every committee and we would all look out for each other's organizations and interest. So if a bill or initiative came down that was unfair to one of the organizations in the coalition we'd fight to shut it down or make it fair. By doing this we were able to get more people involved and diversify our student government. Diversity in every way; both parties or tickets, upper classman and lower classman, Greeks and non-greeks, commuters and on-campus students, thought, religion, experience, interest, racial make up and culture.

In addition, we created a more representative student government and empowered groups of people/organizations that had never been represented or had been under-represented. They now had a say about the things that go on at their school. Being involved and understanding the various levels and functions of student government is one of the most important things you can do for your organization because often times its hard to get the people in student government involved in other clubs/organizations and its hard to get people in clubs/organizations involved in student government. Both are representative of the students. But the student government most certainly needs to be representative of the student body.

Therefore, anytime student government is in session you need to have representation in it, and occasionally attend meetings to know what's going on at the school. Sneaky rule changes and bills are passed over the summer, and in times when there is a lack of student participation, involvement, or people paying attention. This is your **political affairs committee**; they are your representation in the student house/senate and your lawyers if you have to negotiate student court. They are your lobbyists the same way interest groups have representation in the real world. Some will say this is unfair, but in truth, it's leveling the playing field and giving you access to all of the playing cards. No one ever thinks it's unfair when student governments make a ruling or spend money that only benefits its members. This is us playing by the same rules.

And, just as in real politics, be aware of who shows up to support, asking for your vote and asking for running mates, around election time. When you have a successful organization and a successful coalition, people will try to join with selfish reason or break it up. Be wary of people trying to lure your strongest, most popular or most influential members into running with them by catering to their ego. Don't allow any party or candidate to purchase your clubs loyalty with promises of power, funding and appointing your members to key positions. Your organizations/coalitions integrity has to stay intact. If someone wants to climb the student government ladder, it's encouraged. But what nobody tells you is, that the higher you go the further away from the people or cause you get. When you go up the ladder your focus becomes wider. Instead of a certain group, cause or type of event, you now have to be concerned with an entire campus or every member of the student body, or all of the student issues. You no longer get the luxury of singularly focusing on your interest. Don't be fooled into believing the higher you go the more you can do for your organization.

Whenever we would fight for change, back another groups cause, some would often ask, why or how does that affect us? I'd often direct them to this poem about the apathy that existed in Nazi Germany as they came to power and systematically targeted group after group and everyone sat idly by. The poem states,

"First they came for the Socialist,
and I didn't speak up,
because I wasn't a Socialist.
Then they came for the Jews,
and I didn't speak up,
because I wasn't a Jew.
Then they came for the Catholics,
and I didn't speak up,
because I was a Protestant.
Then they came for me,
and by that time there was no one
left to speak up for me."
By **Martin Niemoller**

Through unity, involvement, and cooperation you can have a say in all issue that affect you on your campus and have access to the tools of change and fairness. What started with just a certain event or certain cultural issue, through cooperation has become about all of us. Every issue is now everybody's issue; if one group is being treated unfairly it threatens everybody. It's now about the all-inclusive "WE" instead of the exclusive "They". In the end, we're more alike and want the same things, more than we are different. You've now started to create harmony and tolerance, lessons that go far beyond college.

3. **Learn to get the community involved (Outside of campus)** – One of the biggest mistakes students groups often make when it comes to involvement and attendance, is they severely limit themselves and their cause to just their campus. Groups will often waste valuable time and resources trying to compete and convince students to be a part of their events, even knowing that it's a shrinking pool.

There is an untapped reservoir that many organizations never even think to tap and that is the rest of the surrounding community. Student groups often fail to realize that the students on your campus are not the only people looking for events to attend, causes to support, or things to learn. So while you definitely want to get the students involved, you also want your message to reach as many people as possible. So why think small? You want to continually grow your influence and get your message/ purpose out to as many people as possible. But especially as many like-minded groups as possible, so that you can not only have support but you can also establish working relationships with them. Regardless of whether, it's your homecoming comedy show, a cultural showcase, spring concert, or a community service event, there are numerous clubs, organizations on every level that you can and should reach out to.

It's probably easiest to start with people in the same position as you if your school has multiple campuses why not start with advertising to and trying to get students on other campuses involved in your organization and it's events. If the other campus has clubs and organizations also, attempt to work with the organizations that share your purpose and values, work a deal where you invite them to events on your campus and vice versa. Often times the students outside of the main campus are forgotten about when it comes to funding, involvement, and events. The majority of these resources usually are delivered to the main campus students, so they'll be surprised and appreciative that someone reached out to them. Often times, students at main campuses have a stereotype of acting as if they have an inferiority complex. Break that cycle and began to work with students clubs and organizations at your school's other campuses and locations, reach out to them. As a matter of fact, you could use the coalition and cultural month examples from earlier, and use them to coordinate events, university-wide across all of your school's campuses. You're student at the same school so why limit your network to just the people on your particular campus. It may require a little travel but dedicate your organization to the cause; it'll be worth it.

Another group of potential external supporters you should try to work with exist at other schools. Don't be afraid to reach out to students at surrounding universities, community, and junior colleges. They have organizations you can collaborate with, invite and attend each other's events. Don't limit your cause, purpose or the people you have the ability to influence. On a second note, when you work with students at junior/community colleges, it's almost like recruiting. Many of those students will probably end up transferring to your school in the future. So you now have a chance to get to know them and get them interested in your organization, before they get to campus and you have to compete for them. They come to your school already knowing people with similar interest, having an established network and family to be comfortable with.

There is no limit to how to get the community involved for an event, use your imagination and research the Internet. Depending on what type of student group you have and what type of event you're hosting you can contact community centers, after-school programs, high school student groups, trade organizations, alumni groups, city, state, and nationwide organizations.

As a student leader, I've done events and had church youth groups involved, political parties, county chapter of the NAACP, all the way up to National Aids Awareness Organizations.

There truly is no limit, my organizations have made announcements and invited entire crowds at poetry cafes and jazz venues to similar events being held on campus and we have invited crowds at local comedy clubs to comedy shows at the school. Take advantage of audiences built in and connected to your purposes.

Think about how the university at large already advertises to the community at large for athletic events and university wide events, so why not do the same for your student group.

4.   **Learn to Work a Conference** – One of the biggest opportunities most college students and organizations miss out on is the ability to attend a conference. But most that go to a conference take it for granted and often squander major opportunities that are available for themselves personally, for their organizations and their entire university.

Student often think about the travel, the road trip, the parties and various other events a conference offers. Student often think of conferences as vacations, rather than business trips. It's perfectly ok to enjoy yourself at a conference; executive boards want you to have fun. Conference Committees want you to have fun. A lot of work, sacrifice and battles go into attending or hosting a conference, so executive board and conference committees definitely want you to have fun. There is a designated point in time and a place to focus on nothing but fun at conference. Many organizations often miss some crucial opportunities to learn, network, make crucial contacts and put their organization on the map and spread its cause because they were only focusing on the entertainment portion. The fact that so many students only focus on fun is one of the reasons many schools give groups a hard time about spending money to go to a conference. Many times the school doesn't see the benefits or the return on investment.

When you attend a conference you are in the company possibly of 100's sometimes 1000's of like-minded individuals and dozens of similar organizations. Here is an opportunity to find out what's going on in other corners of the country, other parts of the state, other areas/circumstances of life. Take that time to meet some new people, and share information. Find out what events they do on their campus, you may get some new ideas. What types of problems do they face and how do they combat those issues? Get advice, found out what works for them, what doesn't work. Share ideas, share solutions, get each other's contact information and have your groups follow each other on social media. Give advice and if possible hook up for events, or maybe you can start a nationwide event, several schools do the same type of event on a particular day. Find out what kind of traditions they have? Ask what speakers or performers they've had at their school, recommend some if you've had some. There should be a free flow and exchange of information at a conference. It's ridiculous to attend and only talk to people you came with from your organization. Spread your members out and attend as many of the workshops as possible. If your group is big enough attempt to have representation in all or the majority of the workshops and activities, but don't all pack into one workshop.

And don't be selfish with the information you get at a conference. If you hear something, learn something, or get a contact that another organization at your school could benefit from, share it with them. Go with the mentality that you're attending the conference for others that did not gct the chance to attend. You could represent a coalition of groups and maximize the conference experience. You could even get a number of like-minded groups together and all of the groups attend the same conference. If you go to an informative conference that the groups in your coalition on campus would also benefit from and relate to, invite them to the next one, it'll do wonders for your cooperation on campus.

Talk to the speakers and workshop presenters; get their information, exchange business cards and information with them. Always go to conferences with business cards or some sort of flyer with your information to exchange. Go with the intent of trying to get the speakers/performers to your school.

Here's an example of how we used to work a conference when I was a student leader. Let's assume we attended a workshop and really enjoyed the speaker/ performer. When the speaker was done, if they had a signup sheet we'd put our name on the signup sheet, but also we'd assure to talk to them, shake their hand and exchange business cards, and let them know we were interested in having them at our school in the future. We've started a dialogue, often times at conference it's the best time to book a speaker, speakers/ performers hope to get booked, sometimes they'll give you a deal for attending that conference or for booking early.

Next, if we see that speaker at lunch or dinner, we'd invite them to sit at one of our tables. This is strategic, often times speakers at a conference don't know a lot of people, now you can turn this interaction into a business lunch/dinner and it cost you nothing extra. I'd be doing this at one table, my vice president at another and possibly my advisor at another, we'd have three meetings going on handling business. Or if we were staying in the same hotel, we'd find out if they were taking any meetings, and if we saw them in the lounge or at the hotel restaurant bar, we'd try and have a drink and appetizer with them, that too is a business meeting. By the time we leave the conference we'd have built up a rapport and possibly have a few speakers in pocket for an upcoming cultural month, event, forum, etc. You let the speakers know what type of events you want to do, what you can afford and see if you can negotiate a deal in principle, then keep in contact.

Literally, work the conference, meet as many people, and organizations as possible. Get as much information as possible. Don't just party, try to hook up and be entertained. You'll have plenty of time for that stuff. Don't miss the golden opportunities when they are right in front of you at a conference. You may be able to have a priceless conversation or get some advice from someone you may never have access to again, take advantage. If there is a career fair, that's somewhere you definitely want to be, because those jobs are more likely to respect the experience you have from your student organization. After all, they're meeting you at a student organization conference, so each individual should come prepared for that, bring your resume.

Advice for Advisors

A lot of the things that happen to student organizations and are currently happening are the student's fault. However, there is a percentage of blame and a finger to be pointed at the advisors also. Most students will never say it out loud, but they know it to be true. And most advisors will never admit that they are part of the problem. However, the advisor and student organizations are on the same team and everybody has to share in the blame, success and failures alike.

No one likes to talk about it, but there are a lot of bad and unsatisfactory advisors. Some of the same problems the students are facing in their roles as leaders, advisors are facing in theirs.

There are a number of advisors that suffer from the knowledge and historical problem. It is imperative that the advisor knows the ins and outs, traditions and history of the organization. The advisor has to be an expert and willing to teach this knowledge to the organization. The advisor is the one consistent piece in a machine with constantly changing parts. Year to year consistency lies with the advisor. The advisor helps keep the organization balanced so that it doesn't experience major pole shifts and extreme changes. Maybe it shifts left of center or right of center, but not a change so great that the organization is unrecognizable. Of course, as sensibilities change, so do events and topics. It wasn't as acceptable in the 60's to talk openly about sex, sexual awareness, and sexual issues. But in these times, students talk about them in graphic detail.

To be a good advisor you have to acquire a passion for the organization, its cause, and care for the students and their concerns. The advisor has to be vested in the organization's success. It has to be something you really want to do and really believe in. Don't compromise yourself, if you wouldn't join such a club if you were a student, for whatever reason, then why advise it? It'll just lead to unnecessary conflicts.

Considering at most institutions it's mandatory to have an advisor, student groups don't always get people that possess a real interest or passion for working with students or their causes. Sometimes you end up with advisors that are doing it out of pity, rather than out of a sense obligation, interest or as a labor of love. There are cases of advisors using organizations as fluff for their resumes also, so they can pledge grad chapters or join other organizations.

So it's of great consequence the advisor has a healthy respect for the organization in every way. And it starts with advisors realizing one key essential thing, it's the student's organization, not yours. The organization has to remain student lead, student ran and student controlled. Advisors must know their roles in the organization and be careful not to overstep those boundaries or change those boundaries.

The advisor should not be running or attempting to run the organization, just oversee and guide it. Remember that as an advisor you're the group's greatest ally. Your advisor is your most trusted confidant, and if that trust and respect is broken, it's almost impossible to fix. Your role as advisor is to guide and give the best advice possible, without taking over or forcing your opinion and will on the students. You want to recommend things that help grow, advance and on occasion change the culture. An advisor should foster leadership and unify the organization, mend rifts, bridge gulfs etc. Allow the students to make good and bad decisions, just not destructive decisions that will cost them the club, you your job, and them a possible career. Remember you can't take it personally if they decide to not take your advice or suggestion. The advisor can't be bitter, spiteful or feel rejected. Help the students avoid heartbreak and disappointment. With your consistency and wisdom, you can help them navigate the paths and avoid the traps and potholes if they chose to take the advice. Help them strategize, treat them as adults don't baby them, so allow them to have adult events and adult conversation, as long as it's done with taste and not overboard. They should know and have confidence that the advisor is there for anything they need help with, but not everything. Assure them that as an advisor you won't be a helicopter parent hovering over them, watching over their every move or spying on them on behalf of the administration. Yet, you won't allow them to get in over their heads either. Allow for their organization's history, traditions and principles to be their guide and example, so teach it to them and remind them of it. Advise them on what is a necessary change as opposed to a change for the worse, and how to deal with tradition versus modernization without completely changing the organization. You want to be involved and supporting as an advisor, but not doing the work.

Whether you're a returning advisor or the new advisor; from the beginning of the year set standards, expectations, and inform the group of all their options. In most cases, the group chooses the advisor and they should be empowered to choose whether to continue that relationship or seek another one. For this reason, at the beginning of the year draw up a contract and negotiate the terms of being the advisor. Upon completion of the meeting, there should be a clear understanding of what the group expects from the advisor, what the advisor expects from the group, the advisors availability, and what the advisor will and will not do. List out the type of issues you'd like to have input on and the types of issue that you will intervene on. Inform the group of how discipline will be handled if necessary and the limits of your power. And, if by chance there is a dispute or complaint, inform them of who to talk to. If at any time you chose to dissolve the relationship what's the process and time frame. By giving full disclosure, you build credibility with the group because they now know what to expect and that you're not hiding anything from them, including how to deal with the advisor if there is a problem, so nothing will come as a surprise. Very rarely will anyone in power tell you who to go to, if you have a problem with them when the advisor empowers you to that extent, they gain instant credibility and respect with students.

One other thing, determine whether you're an appointed advisor or a selected advisor. An appointed advisor is someone mandated by the school. If you're an appointed advisor, give the students the option of having multiple advisors. The appointed advisor may be needed for administrative purposes, such as making large-scale purchases or signing off certain types of events, legal issues, or contract issues. Organizations usually have an administrative advisor if a group will be doing things that can have major consequence to the university. If the school is going to appoint a group/organization an advisor, allow the students to pick a general advisor also, someone they trust and can deal with on a day-to-day more casual level. There is nothing wrong with having two advisors. Often times an appointed advisor is a person in the administration or connected to a particular office and it can be intimidating because their often not trusted or bonded with in the same manner as an advisor that the students feel comfortable with and choose for themselves. The last things you want as an advisor is to not be trusted or to have the group fear you. Even with an appointed advisor have a contract; what administrative issues and instances is the advisor expecting to know about, what's mandatory, what types of things will they approve or not approve, what things do they need to sign off on? What things are negotiable, what's none negotiable, how often would you like updates and what are your preferences?

 For example, I dealt with an advisor that wanted updates of the budget monthly and anything she was to sign off on she wanted it at least three weeks before the event in order for her to approve it. Inform the students on what types of meetings you would like to sit in on, what risk you will take for them, what things are you willing to go to bat for and defend, and what things you will not. To be an advisor, you have to be a risk taker because at any point in time things can go from peaceful to chaotic and your personal and business relationships can be negatively affected. If by chance there is a dispute between you and the group, agree on who can be a 3rd party mediator. The third party mediator should be someone neutral, not the other advisor. To ensure that students do not feel they can go to the other advisor when things don't go their way with the other.

It's extremely important for students to comprehend that they can and possibly will disagree with their advisor and that they are allowed to challenge them, but they need to know how to go about it.

Administrators have to remember they once challenged authority and questioned it also as a young person. So please do not take it personal or take a "respect your elders" or "because I said so" stance against student groups because it creates a division that doesn't allow administrators and students to remain open minded, negotiate and work together for positive changes. Most administrators come from a generation where they not only questioned authority; they challenged the system and blew doors off the hinges for us to have the opportunities we have today. However, now that they are the authority and apart of the system, the administrators don't appreciate students rising up against them. Change does not happen by being stagnant and accepting past progress and rolling with the new status quo. Advisors, especially administrative advisors, need to encourage students to be involved and fight for what they believe in regardless of how controversial or lofty the goals, without fear of politics or retaliation, be it from the administration, advisor, or student government.

Administrators and advisors have a huge impact on student's confidence. You don't want to develop a bunch of sheep that are silent, afraid, go with the flow weak leaders; that as soon there is backlash or a challenge, they run and tuck their tails between their legs. Those types of people don't make effective leaders in schools, organizations or out in the real world. And remember you're cultivating young adults for the long term. So as an advisor, be prepared for controversy in all of it's many forms, whether it is the executive board vs. members, the group vs. the advisor, the group vs. the administration or the group vs. the student government.
Be prepared to help your students learn what to stand for, how to do it, and how to pick their battles.

As the advisor, you want to always be the adult in the room and maintain that image and perception among the group. So in the interest of the student maintaining respect for you, you need to always be professional. You can't act and carry yourself like the students and then expect them to respect and understand when it's necessary for you to lay down the hand of discipline. You're to be more of a mentor than a friend. Be careful how you hang with, talk, or joke with your students so that they never mistake the nature of the relationship. It's not a good look if the advisor is out partying, flirting and trying to date people in the organization. It's an unsavory situation. In fact, I know of advisors and organizations that have implemented strong non-fraternization policies, for the advisor, grad assistants, and the executive board members. A relationship gone badly can destroy an organization, a person reputation, and the school's reputation. Advisors have enough on their plate and by agreeing to advise a student group you add on to the plate, don't be your own worst enemy. You treat the organization and students with respect in a business manner and they'll follow suit.

Being an advisor can be extremely rewarding and a challenging experience. It requires sacrifice. We know you're often tired after work, you're busy with your own lives and that being an advisor is extra work that you do not get compensated for. You get extra responsibilities, extra attitudes, extra stress, extra risk and extra things to worry about. But you rarely get enough praise or thanks. On behalf of everyone, thank you for your time, patience, for being friends, mentors, therapist, big brothers/sisters, and parents on occasions.
□

Advice from other Advisors

• - Let your students know that it's ok to make mistakes. The real world is unforgiving. This is the place where they can try and learn.

- Micromanage at a minimum. Help them develop the agenda and simply advise thereafter. It is the student's organization. It is their lesson and experience.
- Hold students accountable. This includes accountability to their constitution, the institutions and the people involved.
-Meet with the leadership and do it often. - **Dwayne A. Hunt**

• Having been an advisor for one of the largest student organizations at a fairly small university, I would offer the most rewarding aspect to be the honor of seeing a strong, continued shared vision over the years. Each executive board serves with a different dynamic, different style and different methods for the organization's success. Seeing the personal and organizational growth makes me feel proud and satisfied. The challenges faced as an advisor for a student organization are to trust the executive board to identify, mediate and resolve conflicts and challenges without hindering the organization, and standing down as the students work through issues and not imposing too heavily on the process. My advice to student leaders communicate with your advisor. Be honest and upfront about what is expected and issues that are occurring. My advice to advisors, trust your executive board to resolve issues amongst them but remain accessible and aware of how the organization and it's members are doing. - **Rachel Mondesir**

Final Advice for Student Leaders (Presidents)

Being the leader of an organization can be confusing and stressful. But it can also be one of the best experiences of your life. Often times being the leader of a student organization is hard for an individual because you are often unprepared and don't know what to expect. You've seen it done, but you don't understand the job or how to do the job until you're in it. Being President of an organization is on the job training at its finest, and as soon as you're starting to get the hang of it and get good at it your term usually ends. No other position on the executive board prepares you for the duties of the president. It's an extremely weighty position and it comes with uncertainty. Not many people can or wish to relate to the amount of pressure or responsibility that comes with it. It's not a job for the weak, frail, unorganized or impatient.

The key to being a good leader is preparing for the position before you are even in it. There are a few things that you should think about and do, before becoming president or even accepting a nomination for president. Before even considering being the leader of an organization, learn as much about the position as you can, and what the day-to-day responsibilities are. This way you will know ahead of time whether you are truly cut out for it, and if you wish to take on this much responsibility. Then, figure out why you want to be president.
You are never truly prepared to be the leader but you must be mature enough and be brave enough to do it.

After an election, especially a close one, find a way to keep the other candidates that ran for office involved in the organization. Those are people that obviously wanted to be involved and wish to be leaders, don't miss your first opportunity to secure future leaders for years to come. Work with those that wish to be involved. A contentious election can rip an organization to shreds.

Keep everyone that wanted to step up involved to show that no matter our differences, we're all working for the advancement of this organization.

Once you become president, **prepare for an onslaught** of things that no one usually tells you about being president because these things don't pop up in the description and most leaders don't really discuss them.

If you're going to be president you can't go into it blind. You need a vision, goals and a plan to execute. A goal without a plan is a wish, and if you don't have a plan, you'll wish you did later.

Often times the role of the president is vaguely defined, so you have to have a plan, a vision and goals so you can work effectively. The executive board will take their cue from you, so you best be prepared to set the direction, pace, and standard for the organization.

Be ready to mature. Being the leader is going to make you a more serious person, it's going to mellow you out, force you to grow and develop in certain areas of your life, very quickly. From day one people are going to be looking towards you for advice, direction, and instruction.

You need to figure out and establish early what kind of leader you wish to be. Do you want to define the position? Or redefine the position? Do you wish to do things the way every other president has done them or do you want to change things a little bit? Do you believe that you are a trustee, in which you can use your own judgment to do what you believe is right for the members and organization? A delegate, where you do what the members want done for the organization? Or possibly, a Politico, where you walk the fine line in between both trustee and delegate? What do you want to focus on and champion for? Sometimes what members want is not what they need or what's best for them or the future of the organization. Being the president means you're required to weigh out these decisions and possibly make the dreaded unpopular decision. The best decision is not always the popular decision. And big decisions are not always the ones of greatest importance. A series of day-to-day minor decisions can totally outweigh one huge decision.

The president is the face and spokesperson of the organization. Fairly or unfairly, everything about the organization and everything that happens regarding the organization reflects on the president; success and failure, good and bad, prosperity and decline. If half of your group decides to be late or not attend the opening ceremony at a conference, people ask, " Who's their president?" Your group gets national news coverage for doing excellent work, people ask, "Who's the President?"

The president is not just the face of the organization, but also the defender of the organization. You go to bat and fight for the group in battles with student activities, university administration, and student senate for example. You're also the diplomat that keeps us out of battles. Don't just be reactionary, occasionally go to student government meetings/ council of student organization meetings etc., introduce yourself as the president, invite them to events.
Don't just show up to the seats of power when you want something or have an issue. Let them know who your club is and what you do on and off campus so they don't assume you do nothing or question what you need funding for. So when sweeping rulings or budget cuts are made, your group can be thought of in a positive light.

 To be the president is to take blame for things not entirely your fault and to take criticism for everything. Being the leader is usually filled with silent admiration and very loud and public criticism, a lot of requests and limited thank-yous, congratulations, or kind words. A great piece of advice, network with other presidents, past and present. You need to associate with other people that deal with or have dealt with the same types of pressure, situations and decisions. You need other people who can relate and give you advice based on experience, and comfort you so that you don't feel alone. A president-to-president discussion can give you major insight or reassurance, especially before making a huge decision.

Be prepared to speak, a lot. From accepting an award, at a meeting with the administration or thanking everyone for coming out to an event, it seems like there is always something the president needs to say or communicate.

Be ready to explain. If anything goes wrong, all eyes are on you and all explanations will be coming from you. Backup and save everything. Be a pack rat of information, paperwork, and proof. Just in case something goes wrong, you can preserve and protect the organization's interests. Whenever possible get things in writing, on the record, noted in minutes, or recorded. Your memory is short and crowded and in times of trouble, no one can seem to find the proof or remember anything that will help you out. Protect yourself. Know and learn the process every step of the way, what are the hold times, what offices have to be involved, who has to sign off, doing this will makes things easier to trace if something goes wrong. But it's also easier to understand how the process works. By knowing this information you know how early and what's the latest you can start. It's easier to explain in the event that someone believes the process is moving too slowly, and it's simpler to teach to others. By knowing the entire process, you can pass on the knowledge to others or teach them to assist you.

Being a pack rat of information can also be helpful for budget purposes. When you go to present and defend your budget, know what your current allocation is and what your organization requested in previous years. Inform how many events your organization has hosted this year. How many events were hosted by all organizations on the campus, what percent of those events are yours? Inform what the attendance at your events were, what number of events were canceled and why? Now you can make a strong case for the budget you are requesting. Explain everything.

Be prepared to have your judgment questioned and to have to defend both yours and other officers' judgment. You always want to be informed and in the know. If you don't know the answer to a question, the next best thing is to know where to get the answer. Even when all is going right explain why things are going good and how to keep them that way.

Being president is a job full of silent admiration, and loud public criticisms. Prepare to deal with a lot of complaints. It's a customer service position. With service being the optimal word.

While the role is not often clearly defined by the constitutions and by-laws, the president needs to be prepared to be flexible. As president, you wear an infinite amount of hats and uphold countless titles. You are a teacher, counselor, parent, sibling, politician, lawyer, and accountant. You're the face of the organization, but you're also whatever people may need you to be, and you'll be shocked at all of the hats you'll wear during your term.

Because so many hats and titles are worn by a president, you have to be solution-oriented and a problem solver, on all fronts, be prepared rather than not. Whether it is how are we going to fund this event or dealing with a personal problem one of your members is having that they want to talk to you and ask advice about. You are a problem solver and there is no shortage of problems and issues that require your attention. Plan for the best and for the worst. For every event, action, strategy, and decisions plan for the 100 % where everything is optimal and goes perfectly and plan for the 0% where everything possible goes wrong. When everyone else is panicking, you can hold it together because you're prepared.

Be prepared to be on call and to serve at any moment, at any time of the day, because it seems that the president's work is never done and there is no shortage of problems and issues to deal with. Presidents get contacted at the weirdest hours. Weekends, personal times, vacations, late nights, are all times when a president could be contacted with an issue or question that needs to be asked.

Be ready to serve. Good leaders serve the people; you are neither a tyrant nor a boss. Being a leader doesn't mean that you're in charge all of the time. Every good leader was once a better follower. Every now and then as the head, you have to go back to being a follower. Sometimes, as a leader, you submit to other leaders if you're working with other organizations, sometimes to the people you serve. Remember the entire executive board serves at the pleasure of the general members. You as president serve at the pleasure of both the general members and the executive board. Meaning, the members possess the power to impeach anyone on the e-board, and the executive board on behalf of the members has the same right. Respect your organization enough and your members enough to not hide the fact that they can get rid of the leaders and the process to do so. As Thomas Jefferson said, ". . . whenever the people are well-informed, they can be trusted with their own government; that, whenever things get so far wrong as to attract their notice, they may be relied on to set them right."

Being president is all about relationships and people skills. Communicating your ideas, wishes and needs are important but equally important, **learn to listen**. No matter how much you know or how much experience you have, you can always learn something from someone else. Pay attention to all perspectives and all opinions. Disagreements and conflicts on an executive board are inevitable, attack the problem, not the individual. Keep bickering, gossiping, and spreading the organization's dirty laundry to a minimum.

The contrary is also important, learn to shut everyone out. There will undoubtedly come a point where there will be too many opinions, too much advice, and too many good/bad options. At this moment, you have to shut everybody out and go with your gut instinct.
You can take people's advice into consideration, but you're going to have to make a tough decision and not listen to what everybody else is saying. Make bold decisions, challenge authority, challenge processes, and ask the tough questions. "Be proactive, not reactive."-
Ancel Pratt

It's easy to be dominant but learn all the submissive and humbling skills also. The problem with a lot of leaders is they know how to be authoritative but they don't know leadership. As a leader, you're going to have to humble yourself and swallow your pride. Learn to ask for help. You don't have to do it on your own. You should not do it on your own; neither can you do it on your own. Delegate, don't try to be a superhero. Do a lot of checking of your ego. There are two types of team leader: people that want to win/succeed and people that want to be the reason for the win/success. It's not necessary to always be the star player, even when it's easiest or most convenient for you to be. Learn to deal with the different personalities of your executive board, and their work patterns so you can put them in a position to shine. Entrust others to work, make the right decisions, be valued team members and get some experience.

Carry yourself differently. Remember that you are the face of the organization; eyes and ears are always focused on you. You represent the organization at all times as the president, whether it is group official business or in your personal time. What you do will be linked to the group. Being a shining example for people to look up to and follow. Lead by example with consistency and integrity.

Don't ask anyone to do anything you would be unwilling to do. People are going to put a lot of faith and trust in you, make sure you put them in the right position. Make sure you walk the talk. People will be willing to work with you and do things for you if they see that you are in the trenches and working as well, not just dictating orders. Know that you will forever be linked to being president. People will always remember and to some degree look up to you and treat you as their leader. Leave them with good impressions.

Don't be afraid to fail and don't be afraid to let others fail. Failure is a part of the process of success. Don't let failure scare you, let it motivate you and hold you accountable. Sometimes you'll learn this lesson and sometimes you have to teach it. For example, it may be necessary to let an event or plan fall through so that the executive board can learn the importance of following through, completing assignments on time, working together etc.

Success and disappointment come with the position. Two things you must learn to do as president are follow up a victory and recover from a defeat. You are the motivator and equalizer for the group. After victory and defeat, you're most vulnerable. Whatever it took to get the victory you have to continue to do because if you rest or celebrate too much you'll lose it. After a defeat you must regroup, retool and encourage everyone to not lose faith or motivation. Remember sustaining excellence is harder than achieving excellence.

Know when you've done all you can, whether that be fighting for a change at the school, an event or idea for the organization or as you're getting ready to graduate and you feel as if you didn't accomplish all you wanted for your organization. Don't dwell on it for too long. There are some things you're just not going to accomplish and some battles you won't win, be proud of fighting the good fight.

Leave your organization in better shape than you inherited it. Treat it like the first rule of medicine, Do no harm.
At worst you want your organization to make lateral moves, but you want to strive for continuous upward progression. Remember, good leadership is not only about what happens while you are in office but also the lasting effects of what happens after you leave office.
Use all the powers of the president to your advantage, to do what is best for the organization. There are some unpopular tools you may at one point or another need to use. Use your veto and ability to table issues, use them sparingly but poignantly. Don't be afraid to impeach/fire people if they are not doing what they are supposed to do, do not allow them to continue shining a negative light on the organization and be privileged enough to continue to hold a position. If they can't do the job, don't be overly forgiving, and afraid to make the decision to dissolve a harmful relationship. It's business, respect your

organization enough to make the smart business move. Many harmful relationships have been allowed to foster because the president did not want to clean house and look like the bad guy only to regret it later. Don't be a pushover.

Don't forget to have fun. It's a lot of work and responsibility being the president. But work hard and play hard. Enjoy being the president, it's still college and at the end of the day, the present day will be the good old days in the future, so enjoy it in the moment.

It's not impossible that everything doesn't go right during your term. Do not be afraid to step away. Life happens. Do not risk your grades, health, integrity or life changing opportunities. Being a student leader can be stressful, don't risk your health. If you feel you're compromising your morals or beliefs step away. Don't forget that you're in college and there is life after being a student leader. If an internship, study abroad, job, a major experience comes, consider taking it. Even if it's medical reasoning, if you've trained and instilled knowledge into everyone correctly, you won't have to stress about trying to stay around to save the organization. Plan ahead so that these types of events don't interfere as much as possible, by no means am I telling you it's ok to take a position knowing that you have an internship coming up that will interfere with your duties to the club. Remember school, life, and family are first.

Be ready to transition. Realize that after being president there is an adjustment period and phase to not being in charge and as influential as you once were. You'll miss it, and be relieved that the pressure is off of you, but for some people, it's hard to not be in control and influential anymore. Realize that you did what you could in your time, and allow the new crop of leaders to have their time. Do not delay your graduation to stick around to serve again or to help out. Do not even think about it. You may believe the organization needs you, and you may be correct, but when it's time for you to move on do so. Nothing good in your personal life comes from holding yourself back. A brand new world awaits you, go explore it, you can still be an influence and help anyway possible as an alumni.

More Advice From Other former Student Leaders

• If knew then what I know now, I would definitely have apologized less and made even more bold decisions. As president or student leader, I would have taken more advantage of the resources we had access to and inspire even more people to get involved. As I have branched out to the real word and join the professional workforce, I have realized that everything we've done, as student leaders were preparations to serve our communities. I would advise any student leader or president to build allies, make friends and establish partnerships with like-minded individuals because more than likely those same people will become instrumental figures and pieces of the future's puzzle. – **Jerson Dulis**

• As the founding president of a NAACP chapter, I remember that at times working together as a team was difficult. However, as the person who was looked up to as the leader, I was careful to not have the appearance of bias towards any particular individual's opinion. When the members of an organization feel like their voices are not as important as others, it stifles camaraderie, growth, and effectiveness, which lead to a stagnating and demoralizing environment. Another point I'd stress is to ensure that projects are delegated to others in the organization. It's not feasible, and rather ineffective to try and carry the load yourself. I was fortunate to have self-motivated individuals alongside me so this made things relatively more relaxed. However, members must feel that the President works as hard for the organization as any of the hardest working members. I do wish I would've known that choosing a great advisor is as important as your fellow board members. – **Kweku Darfoor**

• The advice that I wish I had before becoming a leader is "Don't wait so long to take on a leadership position". I feel like the best time to be on an e-board is before senior year and that senior year should be reserved for internships and finding a job, not planning events and running a student organization. For the presidents: You may never be in this position again. By that, I mean being in charge of an organization, being given money to spend on what you want, being able to make mistakes without it personally affecting your future, is a position that very few people find themselves in. You may never be in this position again, so my advice is to choose a project, a legacy project, be as ambitious and as bold as you can be and go for it!!! Every president needs to have one! - **Roberto Roy**

• Leadership is investing your all into the development of your organization and others. Leadership is not always tackling the minute issues, but taking on all problems with a positive approach. Being able to have others buy into that approach will determine the outcome of your organization and in your personal life. - **Diangleo S. Frazer**

• -Respect the history of the organization/group/club you are leading
-Embrace ideas that are not your own
-Have a clear agenda laid out for meetings
-Communicate your agenda to attendees a few days prior to meeting, for everyone to be prepared and engaged
-Do not lead by blind ambition, but lead by example
-Be humble enough to also do the work you delegate

-"Treat it like a wedding but with a twist; bring something old, something new, something colorful!" – **Deborah F.Roche**

• "If everybody around you is ALWAYS wrong and you think that you NEVER do wrong, something is not right." – **Alex Saint-Louis**

• TEAM - Together Everyone Achieve More "Alone we can do so little; together we can do so much" – **Mona Cius**

• I wish someone taught me to Learn how to effectively deal with the different personalities of the executive board. How to effectively discern between older and newer members [concerning] their advice. Who really cares about the org growth rather than their personal feelings? And I've learned that you are always watched. My advice would be to learn how to take your personal feelings out of decisions for the club, not everything should be taken personally because in the end the club will suffer, think about what the club was created for and what made it last the amount of time it did.
Being president showed me that I was as open-minded as I thought I was. It strengthened my people skills. It brought me out of my shell because being president, you're the face of the org and everyone comes to you. And me being an introvert it really brought me out of my comfort zone. And it put my major to work, studying people and trying to please the masses – **Mikerlande "Mickey" Erilus**
☐

• Outside of [your school's] gates, your organization is the face of the school. Ensure that [your] actions and those of [your] members will not bring the school into disrepute.
-Make sure that you are aware of the policies related to purchasing in the school's name.

-Work with other student orgs and support them as well. It breeds good camaraderie, can make sense financially for joint events and also great for networking

-If your organization is affiliated with] a national or regional body, try to participate in their [events] as well. It can open scholarship and job opportunities for [you] and members in the long run.

-Make sure that amidst all the fun and "college life" that at the end of [your] tenure, [you] did something meaningful. Presidents have to steer their ship that way, especially if it's [an organization] known as a party organization

- And don't neglect your studies. Number 1, you're there for school. Don't waste the opportunity that you, somebody, or whole communities of people are paying for you to have. **– Dayna Smith**

• My best advice to a future student leader is to get the [most] out of the experience as you can. Talk to people, get to know them, get to know their stories. There is nothing worst than a leader who doesn't know the people he/she represents. Get to know your administration, in and out of student affairs. These are the people who will pull strings for you, give you recommendation letters, and shed light on some connections you may or may not know of. When talking to people it is important to always be genuine. Some people can sense when you're not being sincere and you're talking to them to get something out of them, such as a vote. You may want to get into the student leader position wanting to help people out but remember your health and your studies come first. So make sure you manage your time wisely. All in all, get the most and the best out of the experience. In the end, it can be challenging, yet rewarding. **– Collene O'Reilly**

•

• Some advice I wish I had was to take more time for myself. We all know that sometimes when we get involved in organizations we can be consumed by them, in terms of time and energy. We should always remember to take time for ourselves. A long time ago when I was in high school, maybe 15, my best friend gave me some advice that I used as a leader, and still think on to day. He said to me, "remember not everyone is like you, not everyone thinks like you or holds the same values" - so when you are expecting something of someone you must remember that we are all different with a unique set of experiences that make us who we are, we should still have expectations of our members but not always the same expectations that we have for ourselves. – **Roxanne De Freitas**

• - "It's hard to deviate from popular consensus, coming from either your peers or your advisor(s). Don't be afraid to stand-alone and do what you believe is the best thing for the organization in the short and long-term. After all, you were chosen to be a student leader by those that believed you would represent them to the best of your ability!"

-"Don't be afraid of challenges. Your experiences whether good or bad—as a leader now are providing you just a glimpse into what real-world organizational leadership is. Be calm, dependable and most importantly rational in all that you do." – **Kerri Ann Nesbeth**

• Prior to becoming a student leader, I wish I interviewed past presidents or members of the E-board on what their mistakes were and how did they grow from the experience.

- As a student leader expect most of the initial work will be done by your own initiative. Don't wait for someone to give you direction. You should step up and get to work.
- You and the other leaders set the agenda. You control the distribution of the information.
You maintain the history. You set the purpose and direction of the organization.
- Your formal education is the primary reason I am here. Without my ability to succeed academically, I am ill equipped in my social endeavors. Keep the first thing first, be the best student.

Things learned while being president of a student organization:
- Leadership is implied. NO ONE WILL FOLLOW A TITLE alone. The title means nothing if you fail to demonstrate the leader within.
- Treating your fellow students as a mentor, friend, and master. You should demonstrate what a leader is by being in service to your membership.
- Create the Experience and develop culture. This club is not just a place people come to hang out. They want an environment to feel at home. It is not just a meeting, but an experience that created memories and connects them to the organization.
- Give out jobs. Put people to work. If you want them to stick around never have them linger.
- Know the role players. You should get to know administrators, faculty, staff, and other student leaders.
– **Dwayne A. Hunt**

Epilogue

What has happened to our student organizations then? It's obviously not a funding problem. Organizations of the past accomplished more with less and sometimes no school-related funding. There are plenty of alternative ways to get funding, many corporations will help student organizations by sponsoring events, and it's a simple call, email or letter request away. It's not entirely an issue of opportunity. More opportunities exist for students today than ever before. It's not entirely the schools; they're actually more accommodating and are changing rapidly. It's not that student organizations or their causes are out of date, and no longer needed.

The problem lies with the people. Students take for granted how important these groups are and underestimate what they can be used for. This generation is distracted, by all of the advancements, technology, and opportunities they have. They are not aware of all they can do. We've become too reliant on technology; organizations no longer have a personal touch or connection to the people they serve or their cause. We don't pass out flyers, leaflets or booklets anymore; instead, we send an email or a text message and post a picture of a flyer on our websites. We no longer ask people directly to come to a meeting and then walk them to the meeting, we send an invite now, something that may or may not be read. The student organization has become so impersonal, so cold. Social media has become the end all be all rather than just a tool in the arsenal.

It's made many lazy because it's so easy to just complain and be an armchair activist, rather than actually get out, recruit people, and go to the seats of power and not take no for an answer. Changing your picture in support of is not more effective than going to a meeting. Reposting a status is not more effective than setting up a protest or going to an event. This generation has not found it's enough is enough moment, that makes them spring into action.

Students today don't need to fight just to exist on campus. They see so many people like them that they take it for granted. So much progress has been made that this generation only knows one side of the coin. They didn't experience the bad or the transition to a better process. So they are comfortable with the status quo because they often don't know the opposite side of it. They've heard about it, but not experienced being held back or suppression first hand. This generation often fails to realize that the maintenance of freedom, opportunity, and progress is often times more important and harder than actually attaining it. Even when things seem ideal and perfect, continue to be vigilant and continue fighting for progress so that we never have to return to those days of living without.

A successful organization has administration after administration that builds and adds onto the legacy. You measure that based on, did you measure up to all of the previous leaders? Did you leave a mark? Did you enter new territory and further progress towards the mission? Did you operate within your purpose? What did you accomplish of substance? Were the values, principles, and traditions upheld? Those are the things an organization's legacy stands on.

As an individual leader your legacy is determined by how many people did you bring to the cause, how many did you retain? How did you grow the club? There are numerous forms of growth, there's physically (members), financially (budget), stability, credibility, etc. How many protégés did you inspire to step up and become leaders, both in your club and in other arenas? Did you entertain and educate your members? Most importantly did you enrich your member's lives by them being a part of the organization, did you create new opportunities for them?

At every leadership conference and since we were children, we have been told that this generation would change the world and bring about changes to society. It is my solemn belief that we are the generation of change. Change has always been lead through our social organizations and institutions. I believe that it is our responsibility to use our student organizations, our knowledge of social media and technology to our advantage, and use our student organizations for something bigger than what has been accepted and expected of us. Seek out problems to fix. Think in terms of **let's fix that!** Our campus is boring **let's fix that!** We have a lot of general programming, but a lack of cultural programming, **let's fix that!** Why are those groups getting more funding than ours, is it an injustice or are they doing something different? Let's find out and **let's fix that!** There is a lack of awareness in this community, **let's fix that!** Why don't we have speakers, lectures, and workshop presenters at our school like other universities, **let's fix that!** We can spend 10's of thousands, possibly 100's of thousands of dollars in one shot, on ignorance, death, destruction and the disrespect of our cultures and young women, in the name of entertainment for concerts and homecoming. Yet, the budget is too tight to get an educational or motivational speaker, at an institution of higher learning? **Let's fix that!**

These continued tuition hikes and added fees are getting out of hand, let's organize make some noise and let's fix that! Is anyone paying attention to the student retention rates and job placement rates after college? **Let's fix that!**

The amount of power, social capital and influence student organizations have is beyond their wildest dreams. They not only have student government powers like student rules, regulations, budgets, and events. They have university power. Student organizations can sometimes have a say so in who is hired, fired, and promoted at a university if they are allowed to participate in search committees for Student Affairs Staff etc. Off campus, student organizations can affect local, state level, national and international politics. Your organization's sphere of influence is literally the entire world so don't limit yourself. The sky is the limit for what student organizations can achieve. We the knowing and we the willing, can and should be leading our communities and families towards change. We should seek to leave things better for those coming after us than we currently have it. That's true progress.

Once we graduate we can take these same principles that we learn and practiced in our student organizations, and apply them to our professional and civilian lives. We know the politics, now we can apply it. The same networking strategies still apply, I'll go to the homeowners association meeting and represents for all of us, you go to the city council meetings, and we'll alternate on Parent Teacher Association meetings. But when we show up, people know that we are representing for an entire community, and if we hear a problem or recognize a problem, **let's fix that!** They don't want to listen to us, let's run our own candidate for the city council, and let's get our own representation on the Community Redevelopment Agency.

The next generation of CEO's, writers, activist, lawyers, politicians, doctors, teachers, preachers, engineers, economist, deans, poets, inventors, entrepreneurs, and innovators, will all come from somebody's student organization. We can take the same stuff we were doing or should be doing in college and step it up a bit, so we can be an intelligent, informed, engaged, involved and aware community and electorate. The power to change the systems we give so much credit to is in our hands, and it starts with things we learned outside of the classroom in our college student organizations.

Let us be the generation that gets out of our own way, takes our former glory and reinstates it.

www.ingramcontent.com/pod-product-compliance
Lightning Source LLC
Chambersburg PA
CBHW051838040426
42447CB00006B/592